Me and My Dad

Me and My Dad

A BASEBALL MEMOIR

─────────────── · ───────────────

Paul O'Neill

with BURTON ROCKS

Perennial

An Imprint of HarperCollins*Publishers*

A hardcover edition of this book was published in 2003
by William Morrow, an imprint of HarperCollins Publishers.

HarperCollins books may be purchased for educational, business, or sales
promotional use. For information please write: Special Markets Department,
HarperCollins Publishers Inc., 10 East 53rd Street, New York, NY 10022.

First Perennial edition published 2004.

Designed by JoAnne Metsch

The Library of Congress has catalogued the hardcover edition as follows:
O'Neill, Paul.
Me and my dad : a baseball memoir / by Paul O'Neill with Burton Rocks.
p. cm.
ISBN 0-06-052405-7
1. O'Neill, Paul, 1963– . 2. O'Neill, Charles, 1920– . 3. Baseball players—
United States—Biography. 4. Fathers and sons—United States. I. Rocks, Burton.
II. Title.
GV865.O12A3 2003
796.357'092'2—dc21
[B]   2002045242

ISBN 0-06-059579-5 (pbk.)

04 05 06 07 08 ❖/RRD 10 9 8 7 6 5 4 3 2 1

To my wife, or "Sweet Nevalee,"
as Dad called her, whom I met at age five
and who has lived all the games from Little League
to the World Series, November 4, 2001.

To my three wonderful kids,
Andy, Aaron, and Allie, whose lives I hope
to affect as much as my father did mine.

Together you gave me four good
reasons to leave Yankee Stadium
and hurry home.

Love you all.

CONTENTS

————————— • —————————

ACKNOWLEDGMENTS

———————————— • ————————————

Joe Bick brought us together and made this book happen. Mel Berger, our literary agent at the William Morris Agency in New York, sold this book immediately to William Morrow/HarperCollins Publishers and guided the project. Thank you to William Morrow's publisher, Michael Morrison, and to our editor, Henry Ferris. We are also extremely grateful to Mim Eichler Rivas for the outstanding role she played in editing this book. Thanks to Brian Cashman, Michael Kay, Billy Crystal, and members of the Yankees team for quotes and notes for this book.

Keep the Faith

The sun was shining bright on the late-autumn day in 1999 that I rode with family and friends from our hometown of Columbus to the beautiful church in Powell, Ohio, where the memorial for my father, Charles "Chick" O'Neill, was to be held. Out in the wooded midwestern countryside, the leaves had turned and the fall colors were on display—reds, oranges, browns, and yellows. A light wind ruffled the leaves still clinging to the trees and stirred up those on the ground.

Another autumn was coming to an end. The smell of winter was in the air.

Ohio-born and -grown, I am the youngest of the six O'Neill children—one daughter and five sons—who were blessed to call Chick and Virginia our parents, and at thirty-six years old I knew enough about changes in the seasons. Not just in the cycles of nature and in baseball but also in the seasons of life. And yet, even though Dad's health had been on the decline and we knew that the time had been coming when he would no longer be with us, I was totally unprepared for the reality of his being gone. Even in his last weeks, frail as he was, Dad always believed that tomorrow would be a bright day and he would be back on his feet again. He made me believe that, too, impossible though it was. That was part of his magic, part of his larger-than-life persona.

Dad's eternal faith in a golden future was as deeply ingrained in him as was his love for baseball—a game he loved as much as I've ever seen any man love a game. Then again, baseball was less a game to him than a way of life, a set of rules and philosophies, challenges and opportunities that provided order to the universe. It embodied so much of who he was and what he stood for—the old-fashioned American values he learned growing up in the Midwest: hard work, sacrifice, courage, devotion to family and nation, overcoming hardship, reaching for dreams.

According to my sister, Molly, while other kids in our neighborhood were being brought up Methodist and Lutheran, in Dad's house we were brought up Baseball. She had that right. My brother Robert, closest to me in age as the next to youngest, saw Dad's passion for baseball as one of the many ways he liked to live poetically. I could see that, too, how he expressed equal gusto for the small and the great moments—from the simple pleasure he got from eating a hot dog as he watched spring-training practice to the euphoria he felt at his son's team's winning a world championship. It was his celebration, just as he loved crowds, entertaining people, mixing up a batch of his famous secret-recipe pancakes, or cranking out homemade ice cream—filling up the house with his friends and ours, always making everyone feel welcome.

For all these reasons, it came as no surprise during Dad's memorial in the sanctuary of the wood-beamed, light-filled church that baseball people, ex-teenagers who worked summers for him in the sixties and seventies, came up and spoke to me so poignantly, recalling how profoundly he touched their lives. It was just fun to be around him. And when it was time for eulogies, at a pulpit made from a massive stump of a three-hundred-year-old tree, four of my siblings took their turns—Molly, Mike, Patrick, and Robert—braving the emotion in their voices to share heart-wrenchingly beautiful stories of Dad's humble beginnings and extraordinary contributions, all of them ending by putting into words their undying love for him.

Kevin and I were unable to speak. As each of my siblings approached the pulpit, I tried with every fiber of my being to gather my composure, but the more I listened to their remembrances—crying, then laughing, then crying harder—the more of a wreck I became. By the time the four of them were finished, I couldn't say a word. I couldn't face the moment. What they had said and acknowledged meant a lot to me, and I was grateful they had articulated so many of the feelings we all shared. I was grateful, too, that everyone seemed to understand my struggle.

As much as I wanted to speak—had I not been crying inside as if a dam had been broken by thirty-six year's worth of flooding memories—I would have wanted to say thanks to the man who was my childhood idol, my first and last teacher, my coach, my cheerleader, and my best friend. But there was so much more to say.

In some form the lessons learned at his side and the memories contained in the pages ahead are an expanded version of what was in me to say that late-autumn day in 1999.

I speak now, three years too late to make it up to the old tree stump, not in eulogy but more as part of a conversation I continue to have with Dad in my thoughts and in my meditations upon more changes in the seasons. If I could have had one last long walk and talk with the "Old-Timer"—one of my fond nicknames for my father—this would have been it, this walk home together, back through time. "Little Buddy" was my other nickname for him, partly because after I'd grown to the height of six feet four, I'd surpassed his height by five or so inches. But that didn't mean I ever stopped looking up to Dad.

In this open-book reminiscence, as I picture the two of us strolling past the highlights of our baseball journey shared together, my mind easily calls up images of him dragging our Little League field, hitting me ground balls, pitching me slow curves and fastballs. And I can also see him later on down the road, as he sat behind the plate at Yankee Stadium, cheering me on as my biggest fan and loving every minute of seeing his son play in the major leagues.

But if I had to pick any one memory that let me understand, at least fleetingly, what Dad had most tried to teach me, it would be of an event that took place in September 1985.

After what was to me an eternity of roughing it in the minors and working my way up from the basement to the Cincinnati Reds Triple-A minor club in Denver, I was starting to worry. Even though I was only twenty-two, there were guys younger than I was, not as qualified as far as I was concerned, who'd gotten "The Call"—that magical, all-important opportunity to move up to the hallowed ground of the majors. On the other hand, there were older guys I considered top picks for moving up who never got "The Call." Their stories were legion, how and why they'd been overlooked, sometimes because of one or two bad at-bats, sometimes because of a sudden, unpredictable slump. As hard as I worked and as much as my hitting and numbers as a right-fielder were improving, a bad at-bat or, worse, a lost game, had me calling home in a funk.

For months Dad had been giving me the same message: Keep the faith, Paul. "You go out there and win tomorrow" was his constant refrain after a loss. "Get 'em next time! Keep your dubber up!" To him it was never the last at-bat that mattered, only the next one.

But over that summer, I was beginning to have doubts, my patience running thin. What if I didn't get called up? How long was I supposed to wait?

Dad was certain it would happen, any day. Sooner than I knew. Keep the faith, he insisted.

He was right. After a winning game played the night before against the Iowa Cubs, just as Dad promised, the phone rang early in that September day, hours before it was time to go to the ballpark. Before I picked it up, I could have sworn that its ring had a certain jingle of destiny about it. Lucky, that's how the ring sounded. It was "The Call." The Cincinnati Reds, a hundred miles from my hometown of Columbus, were calling me up. I was to become a major-leaguer.

Suddenly all that bus time in the minors evaporated from memory. What truly mattered as I put down the phone, only to pick it up two seconds later to call Dad, was that this signified the crowning moment of all the sweat, hard work, and faith that he had invested in me throughout my life.

I hollered the news over the line as Dad hollered right back. We were ecstatic. I was going to be playing for the Cincinnati Reds, the team I'd grown up watching, the team of the legendary Big Red Machine! The team of Pete Rose, Joe Morgan, Johnny Bench. Getting "The Call" was one of the biggest rushes of my life, and the thrill it gave my father made it that much sweeter, letting me know I was giving back to him what he had given to me for so many years. This had been his own dream, a dream he then passed on to me. And now it was about to become real. For both of us.

Could I make it? Dad's confidence in me and in my abilities was all I needed to take my baseball career up to a new level.

Still pinching myself, I immediately flew to St. Louis to catch up with the team, and the minute I walked into the hotel and saw all the players in their civilian clothes, the reality hit. This is what I'd been waiting for all my life, what I'd been groomed for. Not wanting nerves and intimidation to get the better of me, I tried to combat my shyness by acting cool. It was not easy when I next found myself in a big-league locker room for the first time as a player, then sitting in the same dugout as Pete Rose and stepping up to take batting practice with the team.

This was the stuff of dreams. The ground under my feet at the Cardinals' Busch Stadium somehow felt different. The air, still warm and humid with a St. Louis Indian summer hanging on, was different. Major-league turf, major-league air.

Reds pitcher Ron Robinson welcomed me on board, a sentiment echoed by the rest of the rank and file of the time. The inimitable Pete Rose, a player/manager without peer, appeared to be watching me carefully during batting practice. Wild-eyed, with his shaggy head of hair, he wore an expression that was hard to read, like he wasn't sure yet if I was up to the test. But, rookie or not, I had to believe that I was ready.

During a break before the game against the Cardinals that night, I hurried to call my parents again, telling Dad, "There's a pretty decent chance I'm gonna get into the game." I had a good feeling about it.

Like many ballplayers who are much more superstitious than I am— putting stock in lucky signs, odd premonitions, in visions and dreams— I'd learned to trust certain feelings, for better and for worse.

Dad and Mom didn't need to tell me they'd be watching the game. I knew that they and the rest of my family would be glued to the television set.

For the first six innings, I sat in the dugout. Then, in the seventh inning, Pete Rose summoned me with a nod of his head to the on-deck circle, putting me in to pinch-hit.

My feeling had been right. This was something, my first day with the team. The pressure was on.

Stepping up to the batter's box, I listened for the first time to the roar of the crowd from that vantage point. Baseball has a music all its own, varying at every level. This new music was a sound I loved, much louder and much different from that made by the five thousand fans in the minor-league ballparks, like pounding drums, as if all thirty thousand or more of them were roaring for my first at-bat. Wow.

But there was no time to acclimate. No time to truly take in the moment or to think strategy. Suddenly there I was—in that batter's box with Cardinals pitcher Jeff Lahti bearing down on me. In that split second, my nerves gave way to an adrenaline rush, and, without a conscious choice, out of instinct, I swung at the first pitch and connected with it, right on the button, as Dad would say, sending a hard line drive into right field.

As soon as the ball left my bat, I charged toward first, with seconds to spare. I probably could have stretched the hit into a double had my nervous legs not wobbled rounding first base. I'd have to be content with the single.

My first hit in the major leagues, off the first pitch thrown to me.

In the locker room after the game, there were high fives and back slaps all around. That was the second-best feeling in the world, the sense that the team valued me. The first-best feeling in the world came after I hurried away to call my folks at home.

Dad was beside himself, proudly replaying some of the details he'd observed as he watched me take my first at-bat and as he heard Joe Morgan, the illustrious former Cincinnati Red, call the play.

Imagine, he bragged, getting a hit off the first pitch in a major-league career! "The first of two thousand," Dad promised.

I laughed. Why not dream? But Dad was serious. A true believer.

In this walk back through time and place, that simple but powerful lesson of faith would definitely be one of the first stops along the way. For any kid or father, any family member or fan who ever dreamed a big dream—whether in baseball or in any aspect of life—there may be no greater gift than having someone else believe it with you.

Of course, the real starting place of our family baseball saga came before I was born, even before Chick O'Neill was born—at the turn of the last century in Nebraska, out in the farmlands of America, back in the days when baseball had not yet come into its own as the national pastime.

PART

———

I

1963-1981

ONE

Family Man

Being the youngest of the six O'Neill children ultimately turned out to be one of the luckiest things that ever happened in my baseball career.

But as I was growing up, it was often a double-edged sword, in more ways than one. When it came to learning about family history, being last in line meant I got mostly hand-me-downs, bits and pieces of stories Dad might tell in his offhanded, by-the-way manner, and other, longer versions filtered through my older siblings who, naturally, knew more than I did about *everything*.

But what I did figure out at a very young age was that we had the potential to become a third generation of professional baseball players that had started with Dad's father, Art O'Neill, who played in the minor leagues in the early 1900s. Grandpa Art's father, my great-grandfather John O'Neill, was a Nebraska homesteader who had married Mary Clemens, possibly a cousin to Samuel Clemens, alias Mark Twain. My mother, guardian and patron saint of the part of our education that wasn't about sports, must have been glad that this literary influence in our ancestry on Dad's side was as much in our blood as baseball was. Later that turned out to be the case, when two out of the six of us— Molly and Robert—took up the pen professionally. In the meantime our sports genes were of much more interest to me.

Grandpa Art, born in the late 1800s, grew up in a time when professional baseball was in its infancy. Though the National League had been around since the 1870s, the American League was formed only in 1901; the general public was just beginning to catch on. For a young man like Art O'Neill, working hard, long hours as a foreman in charge of the Omaha Grain Elevator in South Ravenna, playing ball could only be an amateur interest—squeezed into whatever little time was left over in the workweek. But fate intervened when the grain elevator closed for the harvest in 1909, and my grandfather, with a growing family to support, was forced to find a money-paying job for which he was qualified. As it so happened, he was a darn good baseball player and within no time he was making headlines in the April 12, 1909, edition of the *Ravenna Times,* which reported that "Art O'Neill signed for seventy-five dollars a month to play baseball out in Billings, Montana."

Grandpa Art's stint in the minors coincided with a critical change in baseball that took place in 1911, when the adoption of a ball that had a cork center dramatically increased the potential for high-flying hits and home runs. Before that time the so-called dead ball first used in the game limited the frequency of home runs, forcing batters to rely on mental strategy, bunts, and base stealing. With the more aerodynamic ball, a whole new realm of competition opened up, and crowds began flocking to ballparks as never before.

This was the climate in which Art O'Neill honed his skills, eventually dropping out of the minors and going into the dairy business in

Nebraska, where his brood of good Irish stock grew to eight children: Sham, Lucy, Peg, Jack, Russ, Pat, my dad Charles "Chick" (born March 18, 1920), and Clark. All in all, six sons and two daughters. In spite of the brutal winters and blistering summers, seasons that could wipe out the farm family's livelihood, Dad grew up fearless, with a true pioneer mentality, knowing that his father would somehow manage to do what he had to do in order for them to survive and not starve. They bartered, borrowed, and kept the faith, and everyone pitched in. Dad went to work in the corn fields on his family's dairy farm at an early age, the sunburn marks left by the straps of his overalls a permanent mark of pride.

Life was tough, but—at least in the warmer months—the baseball that Dad learned from Grandpa Art provided an escape, something to take the edge off. Baseball soothed the soul, lit the imagination, and provided him with a rhyme and reason to the hard routine of life. It was community and connection, with his family and friends coming together to play games, but it also let him commune with himself— testing the limits of his skills, pushing himself to be better than just good. He strove for greatness, then as later, inciting the rest of us to follow in that tradition.

In the off-seasons, Dad recalled that the entertainment revolved around Friday-night dances, a main course that was a prelude to the dessert—a fistfight out back after one so-and-so insulted the honor of some other so-and-so. From what I could tell as a young boy listening to his stories, the dancing and mingling with the opposite sex wouldn't be complete without somebody later getting in a good shot or two of a fist of five.

Dad led me to understand that whaling on somebody—like one of my brothers, for instance—wasn't to be encouraged. But back in the "old times," folks in Nebraska wore their hearts on their sleeves, and when it came to family pride, Grandpa Art had passed down the idea that if the O'Neill name was challenged, you stuck up for it. Besides, they'd make up the next day, apologize, and be friends again. Dad convinced me that physical fighting was only appropriate when family dignity was in question. And, fortunately, because most of the arguments occurred *between* O'Neills—having to do with who was cheating in one sport or another—I was mostly kept out of any serious brawling.

During Dad's growing-up years, baseball was in its glory days of the Roaring Twenties, when Babe Ruth, the most amazing hitter the country had ever seen, and his New York Yankees revolutionized the sport.

By the time he came of age, Chick O'Neill got a chance to follow his father's footsteps into professional baseball, signing to pitch in the minors. A photograph from the early 1940s shows him on the pitcher's mound, his handsome face reflecting the intensity with which he must have played. From his stance and his rather inscrutable grin, you wouldn't have guessed that he was a lefty. But that was part of his charm. He was complicated—loveable and easygoing while also incredibly passionate, both traditional and old school, yet left-handed from the get-go. He did things his left-handed way, stubbornly and differently. Dad was 100 percent original.

From what I gather, he was on his way up in the baseball world, making all the right moves that would lead him to the majors, when America was awakened by the bombing of Pearl Harbor. Like the majority of professional baseball players and the majority of able-bodied young American males who enlisted to fight in World War II, Dad shipped out, soon earning status as a paratrooper.

Throughout Nebraska, as in the rest of the nation, there were few families who didn't lose sons or fathers or who didn't know someone who gave his life for this country. Devastating though the memories were, and as terrible as it must have been, Dad felt honored by the opportunity to serve, telling us that his war experiences deepened his appreciation for the value of life. In fact, although my father loved every minute of the ballplayer's life—the camaraderie, the fans, the game itself—in later years he was more proud of the fact that he had served his country.

One of his most haunting stories came from his training days in Panama. "My unit was making practice jumps at night," he began, going on to describe what it was like to parachute from cargo planes into pitch-darkness. One night, as they flew out for a practice jump, a commanding officer misjudged the terrain and called for a jump, unaware that he had sent the unit parachuting over water. Dad and a couple of his buddies landed in nearby trees and were saved. The other paratroopers plunged into the water and drowned. The parachute equipment of that time didn't allow any releases. For those men there was no escape. As my father remembered, there but for the grace of God . . .

Like most returning World War II veterans, Dad wasn't bitter about the interruption to his career, even though—as I understood it—he went into the service at a time when most future major-leaguers are ready to hit the pros, the make-or-break time in your early twenties. But, ever the optimist, he came back after a paratrooping injury had ended his military service and prepared to return to minor-league play, hoping to pick up where he left off.

The year was 1945. By November the nation was still in the throes of victory. The war was over. Romance was in the air. The future once again looked bright. Before heading out to California to play in the minors there, Dad stopped off in Columbus, Ohio, where his brother Russ had moved.

Unlike the smaller farm towns in Nebraska where Chick grew up,

Columbus was a state capital, a progressive university town as midwestern cities go, then surrounded by miles of undeveloped farm land—an ideal location to start and raise a family. Dad liked what he saw and made a mental note of it.

Later on that first November night in Ohio, he saw another sight he liked and made another mental note: She was tall and pretty. Smart and educated, too, it turned out.

Had it not been for a terrible accident, they might never have met.

My mother, Virginia, was eighteen years old at the time. She was living in Columbus with her Uncle Clarence, who had raised her since she was a child. Known as one of the richest men in town, Uncle Clarence—who owned the Gwinn Milling Company, which, coincidentally, employed Russ O'Neill—was a prominent figure in Columbus in those days. A self-made man, Clarence resided in a stately Sunbury Road Mansion—with its hundred-yard driveway and a yard that was lined by a white picket fence—and he loved his niece like a daughter. In an era when women were dissuaded from attending college, once Mom expressed her desire to pursue an education, Uncle Clarence was all for it, and she went on not only to earn her college degree but also to receive advanced training as a medical technologist.

On that fateful freezing-cold night, Mom had just come out of the movies and saw above her a red-colored sky while the frantic bells of fire trucks clanged down the streets. Dad and Russ saw and heard the same commotion and ran toward the Gwinn Milling Company's building, which had accidentally caught fire and was in the process of burning down. Virginia took off in the same direction, almost running smack into Chick and his brother, who were outside trying to help the firemen.

It was then that they were officially introduced. Amid the chaos of the fire, somehow the two managed to have an interesting conversation about how Dad had come home from the war and was heading off to California to play baseball. My mother must have told him about her educational pursuits, and at some point he politely asked for her address, saying he'd like to write to her if that was okay. She accepted his pen-pal offer, and the two began a courtship by mail that was to last several years.

And the rest, as they say, is history.

In 1947, around the time that Chick O'Neill was playing baseball in such diverse spots as glamorous Havana, Cuba, and the boonies of east Tennessee, the sport went through probably its most significant change on its way to truly becoming the national pastime. That was the year that Jackie Robinson broke the color barrier and joined the Brooklyn Dodgers, paving the way for other African-Americans and for all minorities—not only in baseball but in every other sport. Though it would take several more years until the ideals of integration and equality were more fully implemented, Jackie Robinson's sheer heroism in opening that door—in the face of terrible racism—not to mention his contributions to the game, cannot be overemphasized. Suffice it to say that his number, 42, has been retired throughout baseball forever. No other athlete has earned this distinction.

Dad never met Jackie Robinson, but he sort of crossed paths with the Brooklyn Dodgers, who spring-trained in Cuba.

That era came up at the dinner table once when one of my older brothers was complaining about the rowdy fans at a game he'd played that day.

The comment reminded Dad of the fans in Havana. This was a

decade before Fidel Castro came to power, back when high-rolling American businessmen and movie stars came in droves to the island that was only ninety miles off the coast of Florida—some for the night-clubs, music, and casinos, others for the sun and the sand. Baseball was one of the hottest things going, and ballplayers were treated as royalty.

The ardent Cuban fans had the unique habit of throwing things onto the field and yelling out at the players. Not just at high points in the game, but throughout. They actually believed that this was their way of participating in the sport. Obviously, when Dad took the mound, he was on notice that he'd better be good. Otherwise, if he stank up the place, they'd let him know loud and clear, in no uncertain terms.

It sounded dangerous to me.

Dad said between bites, calling me by my oldest brother's name, "Listen, Mike, you want to talk dangerous?" This was a quirky habit of his from way back and a running joke at home, how it took him two or three tries before he hit the correct name of whichever son was being addressed, going through the rest of our names—Pat, Kev, Rob, and then, finally, Paul. Being the only girl, Molly usually didn't get into the mix, but sometimes he threw her name out, too.

Dad continued. The most dangerous place he played was down in Tennessee over in the eastern part of the state, then big-time moon-shine country. Like the Hatfields and McCoys, the mountain families that controlled the illegal moonshine business warred with one another and hated outsiders even more, viewing them as suspiciously as law enforcement. If for any reasons they got to thinking you'd crossed them, Dad told us, "You were as good as dead."

Dead?

"Durn right." Fortunately, he went on, he befriended a local sheriff who forewarned him, driving him into the hills and pointing out places to absolutely avoid. The sheriff leveled with Dad and, without batting an eyelash, said, "Never come here alone, or they'll kill you. They'll think you're a government agent, and they'll just flat-out kill you!"

Whether it was that rough-and-tumble existence that got old or just exactly what made Dad decide to give up the adventuring life of a professional baseball player, he never told us. Maybe it was the realization that lightning wasn't going to strike twice and that he'd better hurry back to Columbus and make that pretty gal his wife before his luck ran out. Whatever it was, by the early 1950s he was married and putting down roots in Ohio with a small business of his own. It wasn't the high-level sales job he could have been sensational at, working for any one of the major companies sprouting up in Columbus, but his own subcontracting business as owner/operator of a backhoe—doing everything that could be done with it, from digging gas and water lines to excavating basements. Again, that was his left-handed way of staking out his own claim, the hard way, but he figured it was worth it to be his own boss, and he knew he'd stay busy, well timing his choice for the construction boom of the decade to come.

With a family in the making, Dad never looked back at what could have been, only at the future horizon and the baseball team of young O'Neills he could assemble right in his own backyard. Literally.

Born on February 25, 1963, I was forever cursed—or blessed, as the case may be—by being tagged as the baby of the family. Having a head of blond curls that only later turned dark seemed to add to the image. No matter how much I begged, pleaded, and ran crying to Mom and Dad, my brothers managed for almost five years to keep me out of their backyard batting practice—using the excuse that the "darn baby" was just going to get hurt.

But somehow, miraculously, they eventually relented and started

letting me come out and take some swings, and I was ferociously determined to hold my own. People later wondered where I got my intensity, and I think it can partly be blamed on having to fight my way into
being taken seriously by my brothers. Of course, in those days they just
about laughed me back into the house, but I didn't care. I was so happy
to be a part of the competition.

For almost the first six years of my life, we lived at 304 East Schreyer
Place in a three-bedroom house, a 1940s-era model that was originally
built for servicemen returning from World War II. Many faculty members from nearby Ohio State University lived in the neighborhood as
well, as did some of the Batelle scientists who worked in cancer
research.

The thought that we had outgrown the house never occurred to me.
Five boys in one bedroom with bunk beds? As far as I knew, that was
the coolest thing in the world. One big party all the time, the five of us
horsing around until late at night—we had a blast!

Not long after I started kindergarten, I realized that there was only
one thing missing in our bustling household that reverberated with the
Rolling Stones blaring from one window and the Beatles from another,
as softballs, baseballs, tennis balls, and whatever else we could find to
hit with a bat went flying through the air. What we really needed was a
puppy!

Fatefully, my parents didn't refuse me, and the two of them located
a family in the neighborhood whose poodle had just had a litter. They
turned out to be the Davis family, whose five-year-old daughter,
Nevalee, was to have a most important place in my future. Mom and
Dad went to see the poodle puppies, befriending Pat and Forrest
Davis, Nevalee's folks, although they didn't return with a puppy.

"Poodle?" Dad quipped. He had bigger dog types in mind, so we ended up getting a couple of Great Pyrenees at our new house on Cook Road. Imagine an all-white Saint Bernard! Meanwhile, Mom and Mrs. Davis arranged to carpool, since Nevalee and I attended the same kindergarten.

Even at five years old, I was taken by Nevalee. Sweet, pretty, and smart, she was the girl next door—almost literally.

Then again, I wasn't spending much time dreaming about girls, not at that age. My dreams centered on sports in general and baseball in particular. This wasn't just my preoccupation. It was the O'Neill tradition.

In some large families, parents can tend to be worn out by the time they get to their youngest, after expending so much of their energies on their older kids. That wasn't the case in our home. Remarkably, Mom and Dad had an endless abundance of energy, love, and attention to shower on each of us. It was as if the more they gave, the more they *had* to give. As far as Dad's imparting his baseball knowledge and training to each of us—including Molly, who played for a few years in a girl's softball league—rather than tiring out, he increasingly improved upon the science and art of his coaching abilities until, by the time he got to me, he was a Ph.D.

After long, demanding hours of work—often with stressful deadlines, juggling different job sites, getting dusty and dirty, dealing with tasks that were physically taxing and emotionally challenging—instead of stumbling home and collapsing into an easy chair, he saw his return to his family as the beginning of his real day. Dad came home ready to play, not ready to rest. The moment his big truck pulled into the driveway, I'd run to the window and watch him leap out of the cab, grab a basketball, and take a shot at the hoop in the yard. He kept taking shots until he sank one, and then he'd walk on into the house to get ready for whatever was on tap. It might be anything from practicing ball in the backyard or heading off to coach Little League or, in colder weather, being part of whatever other sport one of us was competing in: hockey, basketball, football, tennis—you name it.

Chick O'Neill was that rare individual who didn't suffer if the phone bill hadn't been paid or the backhoe needed replacing, or if a job had fallen through and grocery money was limited. As long as we had a baseball or some other game, everything else would take care of itself. It did. With all the clothes, school supplies, and especially the sports equipment the six of us went through, he never worried that he couldn't provide for us. Whatever he may have wanted or needed for himself didn't matter; his wife and children came first, above everything else.

Dad was unsinkable. He woke up singing every day. His theme song? "The Sound of Music." Dad loved that movie with its good family story of the singing von Trapp family. *"The hills are alive with the sound of muuuusic . . . ,"* he'd hum as a typical good morning. After he hummed it about into the ground, my mother firmly interjected, "Chick, that's enough."

Dad's second-favorite song, believe it or not, was "Hey Jude." Molly played it over and over so much in that 1968 era, Dad decided, "If you can't beat 'em . . . ," and then he woke up singing that as well: " . . . *take a sad song and make it betta-er-er. . . . "*

Despite all the ways that I aspired to be like my father, I learned early on that it wasn't something you could do to just wake up and decide to be carefree. I wasn't like that. And yet to have him as such a soothing force and guiding hand certainly helped me cultivate my own breed of optimism.

"Ted Williams," Dad said to me one June evening at a practice field in the neighborhood when I was all of six years old. We'd finished some fielding drills, and he was getting ready to pitch to me as I set my feet and crouched into my left-handed batting stance, feeling the weight of the bat resting on my left shoulder and lifting it slightly. "You remind me of a young Ted Williams."

I looked up at him and grinned. Compliments, then and now, embarrassed me. Besides, to be compared at that age to the famous left-handed hitter "Teddy Baseball," the Boston Red Sox hero, one of the all-time greatest hitters, who'd left to fight both in World War II and Korea, playing from the 1940s all the way to 1960? Ted Williams who homered on his very last at-bat at Fenway Park?

I gave Dad a look that said, *Yeah, right.*

No, really, Dad insisted. The way I held my bat reminded him of Ted Williams.

Another day not long after that, he followed up his earlier remark by walking up to me and putting his hand on my shoulder, peering down into my eyes, and saying, "You're going to be a major-leaguer one day, Paul."

For all I knew, this was a rite of passage, a comment he'd made to each one of my brothers—each of whom had tremendous baseball talents and professional potential. After all, I was only six. Didn't all fathers say that to their sons? But there was something in Dad's eyes, a magical gleam, that made me feel . . . who knew, maybe he was right? Maybe that was going to be my future?

For a few weeks, I put it out of my mind, realizing I had a lot more growing up to do before I set my sights on any professional career. But when, that very summer, Dad announced that he and I were going to drive to Cincinnati so I could see my first major-league game—the Reds against the Pittsburgh Pirates—I couldn't get the dream out of my head.

Entering the stadium at Crosley Field solidified my ambition, then and there. It was like walking into a cathedral. Even though the ball-park is no longer where the Reds play, that first image has remained with me since: the majestic, pristine baseball diamond, the sheen of the freshly dragged and lightly watered red-brown dirt, the emerald green of the lush grass outfield, the small rise of the hill up near the outfield wall that was lined by huge advertisements and logos, and the brilliant white lights illuminating the stadium.

Bursting with excitement to share this experience with me, Dad got us there early so I could have a chance to get an autograph or two before the game. I was determined to get an autograph of the Pirates' stupendous right fielder, Roberto Clemente, number 21.

Dad led me down to the tunnel of the visiting team, where fans were already ten deep, but try as I did to weave my way through the crowd to get close to Roberto Clemente, the Pirates were soon out of the tunnel and filing into the dugout. There was to be no autograph for me. I was heartbroken and in tears.

Dad reassured me. "I'll see what I can do," he said, patting my back, cheering me up enough so that we could return to our seats and enjoy the game. The awe on my face while watching must have been enough to inspire him to take a photograph of me in my Reds jersey standing in the upper deck, posed in my left-handed batting stance with number 21, Roberto Clemente, in the background down on the field. Better that than no autograph, I figured.

But Dad had another plan. At one point he left and returned shortly afterward with the autograph—Roberto Clemente's name written hur-riedly in script!

I was overjoyed, too thrilled to sleep on the ride home, mentally replaying the highlights of the experience, anticipating my brothers' reactions. But when I came in and proudly presented them with the autograph of the great Pittsburgh Pirate, I was greeted with mocking laughter.

"Dad wrote that!" Robert said.

"No way."

"Dad wrote that!" Mike, Pat, and Kevin echoed.

My brothers had probably been through something similar, but I wasn't ready for such a loss of innocence. It was just like telling me there was no Santa Claus.

I didn't want to believe them. Could it really be a counterfeit Roberto Clemente autograph? Why would Dad fool me like that?

I was crushed. Only later did I recognize that Dad's motivation for scribbling that name for me was from pure love. He didn't want to see me upset. He wanted to make me feel special.

The fact is, he succeeded.

And in those few hours of being touched by fame, something special about the number 21 settled into my psyche, somewhere in the back of my mind.

Some might say it was prophetic. But in all honesty, I had no inkling that it would be my own major-league number one day.

·

The House That Chick Built

Though Dad was responsible for teaching me the fundamentals of baseball that would last me my career, my brothers got continuing credit for whetting my appetite for winning—especially once I was admitted to the brutal battles of our backyard home-run derby.

That coincided with a significant move we made in 1968 as a result of my parents' years of hard work—with Dad's business and Mom's job working as a medical technologist at Mount Carmel Hospital. After deciding it was high time to move the family to a more spacious house, they found the ideal setting at 1323 East Cooke Road. Our new home was a six-bedroom, stone and stucco ranch-style house with a pair of two-car garages, surrounded by three and a half acres of beautiful property. The only drawback for me was that, because the houses in the area were more spread apart, there were fewer kids my age around, so I depended all the more on my brothers for playing sports and other activities.

But with what Dad had up his sleeve, we were never in need of something to do. We had barely unpacked when he went to work creating what was to become any sports enthusiast's dream come true—a backyard complex that could be adapted for just about every sport we decided to take on.

That backyard was the best training ground for any future professional athlete, and those home-run-derby games were especially ferocious. If the competitiveness between Yankees Mickey Mantle and Roger Maris to overtake Babe Ruth's home-run record appeared intense, the O'Neill backyard competition might have seemed even more extreme. Winning was *everything*. I was desperate to beat my brothers, to show them what I was made of. They wanted to destroy me.

During one-on-ones at basketball, it was blatant—any one of my brothers coyly letting me get ahead, just so he could come back and cream me to see the look of frustration and agony on my face. Dad tried to give me some perspective, laughing most of this off. He'd been a younger brother once, too.

But the home-run-derby atmosphere was merciless. For those hours after school or on weekends, our true brotherly love took a backseat to rivalries as serious as those when I later wore the pinstripes and took right field in the Bronx.

Losing or striking out with the bases juiced could make me crazy. Some kids learn to laugh it off. Not me.

A board in the corner of our fenced-in backyard area represented home plate. Whoever was pitching stood forty feet away winging tennis balls, no holding back because I was the youngest. The right-handed hitters had a big advantage because of the open space in left field, while the left-handers had to contend with our imposing maple tree, which often acted as a fielder, snaring balls in midair with its mighty branches. If the tree got hold of one of those towering drives and knocked it back down onto the ground, guess what? It was an out. As a left-handed hitter, I had to learn to hit the ball to the opposite field to stand a chance, and so the game taught me early to go the other way.

Once I made that adjustment, my brothers started bringing it even faster, trying to intimidate me. At first it worked, but I soon realized that the faster the ball was coming, the farther I could hit it, and before long I was smacking those balls about two hundred feet for a home run.

When I did, you'd think they'd cut me a little slack for proving myself. But no. "Beginner's luck," they'd scoff. When I surpassed beginner status and was on the side with the lead, my brothers who were playing on the losing side would accuse us of cheating.

"*You* cheated!" I'd accuse right back.

Who got lucky and who cheated, with tears filling our house almost daily, was an ongoing matter of justice. Our backyard was nonstop do-or-die drama, a place where, if I lost in anything to my brothers, I had to go to the dinner table and live with it, putting up with their postgame trash-talking through the whole meal. If I argued my case, it could last late into the night in our bedroom, with the five us going at it until Dad, hiding his amusement, settled everything by telling the losers to just go out and "beat 'em the next day."

Tomorrow never came soon enough for me. The fact that it was going to take several more years of tomorrows before I could compete at the level of my brothers—Mike, Pat, Kevin, and even Robert—was too much to think about.

Our backyard, together with baseball diamonds in nearby parks, became a kind of school for me, where Dad taught me everything he knew about the game.

Before practicing with me over at the parks, he would first get out on the tractor and drag the field, his strong baseball-playing hands that ought to have finished for the day devoted to perfectly manicuring the diamond for his son's benefit. He knew how to drag the dirt and water it just lightly enough to produce the sheen of the major-league ballparks—that nice sheen of brown dirt that every kid, young or old, who has played this game knows so well. If someone had been flying over the ball field in a small plane or helicopter, they would have seen a perfect baseball diamond and a handsome, sturdy, sunburned man working the field over with untiring love.

Sometimes I helped, following along. Those memories are vivid: the sight of the dust rising in the air around us, the smell of the freshly cut grass, the sound of our feet kicking up the dirt mixed with the buzz of the insects, the two of us quietly just spending time together.

To be a kid of seven, eight, nine, and to be able to play on a field that was dragged and watered and ready to go—much like the field at Yankee Stadium—was the ultimate. It was a gift of epic proportions.

By the time I started Little League, with Dad as coach, my friends and I were practicing and playing well over our heads at those ages. The field made all the difference between the lines.

Unlike the irregular heights of grass in most ballparks around town, our outfield blades of grass were just the right height. Dad knew how to cut it so that the outfield looked full and lush while still playing evenly. That way those hard-hit grounders took normal hops. Nor were there any of the usual little hills and valleys and gopher holes that the typical Little League parks have in their outfields. As a result of these perfect conditions, I could run my heart out to catch a fly ball or a sinking liner and not miss a stride.

Sliding into second base, I didn't have a rough slide that burned my legs, but a nice smooth slide like in the big leagues—the dirt on the base paths was that perfectly drawn. The confidence this allowed me whenever I slid into second or third base became as important as knowing *how* to slide.

Playing on that level, compared to what most kids played on, made a dramatic difference. Ground balls hit to third actually went to third, not over the third baseman's head. Whenever a ball was hit to short, or second, we never had to wonder if it would continue to roll through our legs or take some nasty uneven hop—the kind of erratic jumps you get in most sandlot ball.

Dad and I also had the luxury of grabbing our gloves and heading into the backyard. When he wasn't around, my brothers and I had other options, from baseball in the home-run-derby area to basketball on the court that we could use most of the year as long as it didn't snow and, for the coldest winter months, hockey on the homemade ice rink. For a bunch of sports-crazed kids like us, this was paradise. Thanks to Dad, we were able to grow up sharing our sports memories of this ultimate backyard athletic complex—a living testimonial to our father's love for us.

With all that easy Ohio farmland, there was now only one thing that, to me, seemed to be missing: a pony!

For weeks I'd been bugging Dad about how neat it would be to have a pony grazing out in the backyard, until time passed and I'd almost forgotten about it. To my delight, he arrived home one evening with a handsome Shetland pony that my brothers and I promptly named Tonka. He came complete with a buggy to pull!

Apparently Dad had been passing by a farm in the vicinity and had seen a sign reading PONY FOR SALE and had picked him up for me.

Turned out that Tonka, who looked like he ought to be a friendly toy pony, had an attitude problem. He was *mean*. Adding to the general fun and commotion, he ran around crazed half the time, causing his share of trouble.

Dad really amazed me one day when he figured out that Tonka, who suddenly was in a great deal of pain, had a bad tooth. Something had to be done. Rather than spend the time and money to haul Tonka to the vet, Dad's solution was to get out a pair of pliers, put the pony in a headlock, and pull the tooth himself. Tonka felt better immediately, but he still bit anyone, given the opportunity.

I was in awe, standing there and witnessing my father's resourcefulness. In my eyes he was a man who knew how to overcome any obstacle, who had the answer for every problem. To me there wasn't any challenge in the world that my dad couldn't face and conquer.

Yet the things he did so remarkably he never did for the fanfare; they were done for our well-being. Whatever happened, he demonstrated, it was important to do the best that you could, to give it your all. There's no doubt that my desire to do well in sports and to do my best in other areas stemmed from those values.

Chick O'Neill did nothing halfway. Whether it was creating a sports complex in our backyard or cooking up an army's worth of pancakes every Sunday, he lived life to the hilt. After he'd worked six days a week, up at the crack of dawn every day, Sunday was the one morning he had for himself, and his relaxation was to cook breakfast for us. There was a great music to the rhythmic clicking of his fork against the aluminum bowl as he mixed the eggs and perfected the consistency of the batter to make huge, griddle-size pancakes. Dad insisted to us, "You want to grow tall, you'd better eat up." Obviously, he was right. He knew the recipe for making people tall!

When the pancake feast was winding down, there was always some batter left over that he used to make truly Olympic-size pancakes that looked like giant Frisbees—testing the bounds of human appetite.

The Sunday pancake tradition was such a significant family event that even Tonka got in on the act—hanging out by the window waiting for his pancake. My brothers and I cracked up as we threw the big steaming Frisbee pancakes out the window and the pony caught them in his mouth.

Each season brought with it a different memorable celebration that Dad orchestrated. Summer was synonymous with baseball and everything that went with it. My days revolved around the typical summer fun of playing outside, then practice and games, starting in the morning and lasting until night fell. At the beginning of each summer season, Dad made sure that all of our equipment was the best, and his bringing home my first baseball glove stands out as another important rite of passage.

Without being told in so many words, I understood that this was a big deal. From then on I took great responsibility for my glove. It stayed with me most of the time, stored in a special place in my room. Dad showed me how to break in a glove properly—not by soaking it in water but by putting some glove oil on it, with caution, and then playing with the glove until it broke in comfortably. As there was no glove oil around, I was encouraged to be resourceful, and I took some Wesson oil out of the pantry, and applied it, and played with the glove until it felt comfortable.

After using it to play catch, I'd immediately put it away right afterward—taking pains never to leave it out exposed to the rain or other harsh elements. To this day I still have among my trophies at home the glove I played with in the 1970s—in the same shape that it was years ago. At one point, when it needed restringing, I used a piece of wire clothesline to sew up the pocket.

Along with new baseball equipment, summer also brought the homemade ice cream that made us go nuts as Dad set up the old-fashioned churning machine and the fresh fruit for mixing into it and the salt packs around the machine. Part of the fun was helping turn the crank. Those days with my dad seem like they were yesterday, made the more special because of the time he invested in something that gave us enjoyment.

My father cared a lot about these ordinary father-son moments in life. Me, too. There was nothing better than being eight years old and having real lemon-peel, orange-peel ice cream that made my mouth water like crazy.

Ohio summers could be miserably hot, especially because we didn't have central air-conditioning in the 1970s. My brother Robert used to joke that the summers were so hot without air-conditioning that he could shower at night and jump directly into bed without really drying off. So, after a day of playing catch when it was ninety-five degrees outside, humid and sticky, a bowl or two of fresh, homemade ice cream was heaven.

After games or rigorous Little League practice, there was also the option of stopping on the way home at our frequent hangout, Dairy Queen, where, after a thrilling win, us kids would line up at the outdoor window to order the soft-serve ice cream, sundaes, and my usual—a chocolate shake. Meanwhile, our parents took the time to get together and talk about the game or what was happening in their lives. What a great feeling—nine o'clock at night, traces of light still in the sky, but the air finally starting to cool, a chocolate-milk-shake ring around my mouth. Life *was* perfect.

Then there was our local favorite—Knight's Ice Cream Shop. Our whole family loved going to Knight's on Indiana Avenue. My mom used to order a chocolate soda, made with seltzer, vanilla ice cream, and chocolate syrup, while Dad and I ordered the thick chocolate shakes.

One evening when Dad and I were coming home from Little League practice and we stopped in to Knight's Ice Cream Shop, both ordering the regular, I remember him draining the shake down, smacking his lips together, and sighing. "You know, Paul," he said, "I'd rather have a good chocolate shake than a beer any day!"

The implications didn't occur to me until I was older. In his subtle way, he was really teaching me, I found out as a teenager, clean living by example.

Summertime now and then gave me the chance to tag along with Dad to work and help out on jobs. When I was little, there wasn't much I could do, but as I got older, he showed me how to shoot grade to keep it even, paying me ten bucks for the day. Watching Dad in his professional capacity gave me more insights into his work ethic, how it was important to him to make sure everything was perfect—that, for instance, if they were digging out the foundation for a basement, everything had to be even, especially the walls. He had an eye for detail, making sure everything was checked and rechecked, and he took the extra time to satisfy everyone, especially his own high standards.

It meant all the more as the years passed, when I realized that part of his choice to have his own business rather than work for someone else for a higher salary was to have the greatest flexibility to spend time with his family. Dad truly believed in his heart not only that his way of living was the right way but that he was the richer for it, richer because he was able to watch us grow up and be there for us—whether it was for school or for life-altering decisions.

He wanted to see me play ball, not hear about it. He wanted to buy me a thick chocolate shake in celebration, not just give me some money and send me off.

People person that he was, if any friends or business associates wanted Dad's ear, they got it, but we were the first priority on his list. He refused to miss out on fatherhood—from the highlights down to the smallest of events, like watching me practice throwing the fastball, cheering us boys on to sink some three-pointers and, of course, coaching Little League.

The baseball diamonds around the various Ohio cities were like etchings on our family wall, monuments of the good times and the bad. Over time, each diamond came to hold a memory for me—the victories, the losses, and the downright ugly games.

As I moved through elementary school, more and more baseball wasn't recreational in the sense that swimming and riding bikes were. While it *was* a form of recreation, I had begun playing with a purpose, a purpose to improve and, thanks to the O'Neill competitive spirit, with an increasing determination to win.

I should point out that when we weren't playing against one another in our backyard, nobody cheered louder than all the O'Neills did for each other. Wanting to win was about family pride, about not letting down my team, my father or my brothers, my mother or my sister. They never put pressure on me. But I did, from Little League through PONY League into professional baseball. Nobody takes the blame for that. The pressure came from me, myself, and I, my individual makeup.

That determination probably fueled my desire to soak up every bit of knowledge Dad had to offer me. Because of his natural talents and his background, it was as if he had opened up an old baseball locker and we'd both stepped inside for a unique journey that would last a lifetime.

In our backyard this really began with his teaching me the fundamentals, starting with pitching. He used to throw me a great left-handed curveball. With that old-time motion, the pitch was a classic that involved his whole body in a big, rocking movement, with the windup and follow-through and, when all was said and done, a long, looping curveball that crossed the edge of the plate.

When it came to the art of pitching, nobody had a better sense of *how* to pitch than my dad. He knew how to pitch inside. His finesse didn't allow for anything like the wild throws some pitchers get off these days that either go three feet behind a batter's backside or knock the batter down. Dad was as in control on the mound as he was off the field.

The metaphor for him was that, in life as in baseball, you can't go back and do it again. You have to keep moving forward.

Good pitching started with the grip, Dad explained. He showed me how to grip the ball in my hand to have maximum control. Then there was the throwing motion. With practice I caught on and eventually attained a formidable ability for a kid. I could throw a two-seam fastball and a slider.

But that wasn't enough. Dad could make the ball move like a wizard. How in the world he did it was beyond me.

Then he schooled me, and before long my pitches were breaking just like his, and it was as if we were both locked in, mind-set and all. It still amazed me each time the ball crossed the plate, until it became second nature and I could stand on the pitcher's mound, grip the ball, and throw it the way I wanted.

In Little League, Dad was intent on teaching all of us to throw the ball overhand. Staying on top of the ball was the key. This was important both for developing baseball skills and for preventing injuries. Dad thought that if a kid's arm was injured early on, it could affect him all the way through high school. The parents of the kids appreciated my father's emphasis on safety, knowing the care he took so that none of us got hurt.

Dad was equally as passionate about having us all learn how to bunt effectively. Naturally, when we were more concerned with showstopping at-bats, the need for good bunting wasn't our priority. Dad promised that it would come in handy later on in my career, and he was proven correct. I can still hear him saying, "Paul, don't jab at the ball. Just get the bat out in front of you, but make sure you keep your eyes level with the ball."

These fundamentals seemed simple enough at the time, but, to my surprise later on, even as a major-leaguer, I would see guys coming up from the minor leagues that still couldn't do this stuff right. I'd wonder what in the world they were teaching them down there.

There was also baserunning and savvy, the mental side to the game that Dad wanted me to understand from the beginning. Baserunning he considered to be practically a lost art. The secret was to make sure to hit the bag with our right foot so that we'd be able to push off and get a better jump. In Little League there were moments during a game on a huge base hit when I'd be rounding third, attempting to score from second base on that hit, and after so many hours of practice I could hear my dad's voice inside my head telling me, "Hit it with your right foot! Hit it with your right foot!"

Later, when I played in the major leagues, his voice was still there, and in my opinion there were times when running the bases properly saved many a ball game. The reason is that, by hitting the bag properly, you give yourself that extra edge in running that is so critical in a bang-bang play at the plate when you have to go into your slide and every second counts.

Dad taught me how to steal bases and how to be a base runner against a crafty pitcher. He demonstrated to me how to break on pitches when I was on first base. His theory was that a base runner should try to run on curveballs and change-ups because those pitches are slower ones and the balls have a tendency to break down and end up in the dirt. The catcher can't get off the same throw that he normally would if the pitch were a 95-mph fastball, shoulder high.

One of the most important pieces of guidance Dad gave me was the value of hitting for average. Hitting home runs brought the glory and the crowd to its feet, all right, but winning was about consistency throughout the game. Since I wasn't used to hitting loads of home runs, he convinced me that if I could help my team win a game 3–2 or 2–1 on a timely single and some heads-up running on the base paths, then I was doing my job.

A winner, in Chick O'Neill's book, was steeped not only in baseball fundamentals but also in the basics of good sportsmanship and fair play. Somehow the skills sank in before the good sportsmanship did!

Looking back on those days, I can see that what he passed along to me was invaluable. His passion was infectious. It was what made him tick, what had made him the happiest as a kid. And passing it on to me was not a way to relive his childhood through me but a way of sharing what he had learned with the most eager of students.

My father coached two of my older brothers—all five of us played on very competitive Little League teams—and he was consistently fair with all of his players. He never played favorites, nor was he an oppressive stage father. Of course, nobody needed to push me. When I kind of sneaked in and practiced with my brothers, it was not because Dad forced me to play on their level, it was because I wanted to be there. My brothers welcomed my playing with them, too, and, in so doing, helped me become a much better player. As with anything in life, getting an early launch can make a difference in the long haul.

Truthfully, I loved baseball so much that the season never started early enough for me. Whenever each season ended, I was soon counting the months until spring training. In the dead of winter, while it was freezing cold outside, with everyone bundled up, wearing black rubber boots and carrying shovels to dig out from under a foot and a half of snow, I was inside getting psyched for the next Little League season.

Whenever St. Patrick's Day arrived—always a festive occasion for an Irish family like ours, including the fun I can recall while marching in the annual parade with the Shamrock Club through downtown Columbus—I was celebrating also because I knew that winter was over and baseball was just around the corner.

Going to Roush Sporting Goods to pick out my uniform with my dad was a big trip for me, an event I anticipated with pride every year. Along with a new pair of tennis shoes and a new pair of socks, we'd select my baseball uniform—polyester double-knit jersey and pants. Little League or not, this was no ordinary uniform. It was an authentic jersey that made you proud to pull it over your head and wear it. Wearing it represented my pride in my team, and it connected me to the whole father-son experience, the bond we had forged in baseball.

The 1973 opening-day game in Little League, when I was ten, was a game that made all that long waiting through the winter worth it. We were playing our archrivals in Hilliard, Ohio, at night under the lights. The Hilliard Colts were coached by Harold Butts, and their pitcher, twelve-year-old Dallas Sharp, threw hard, really hard. He was the Roger Clemens of our league!

Pitching for our team was none other than my brother Robert, who was almost as old as Dallas Sharp and just as tough to hit. In those days in our league, ten-year-olds and twelve-year-olds were allowed to face each other, something that's less common nowadays.

The game was close, but at the top of the sixth inning—our games were six innings long—we were down a run.

I led off with a double. I was moved to third and then scored on a wild throw to tie the game for Robert. Tying the game was great, but the fact that I'd helped out my brother made it even better. "Big Red" McFerren—a six-foot-tall twelve-year-old on our team who towered over everyone and lived to joke around—suddenly marched up to the plate like he meant business and hit a big home run. We pulled ahead and went on to win 2–1.

Because of sharing the win with Robert, that game has remained as vivid as any I *ever* played in the majors.

Sometimes our older brothers stepped in to umpire our team's games when, for one reason or another, regular umpires weren't around. The unwritten O'Neill law was that brothers be impartial as umpires and not play favorites. This didn't stop Dad from riding Mike just as he would any umpire if Mike made a bad call. Good and bad calls alike, Mike was still taking time out of his schedule to be helpful, so I appreciated it. He could have been having fun with his friends, but he was doing this out of brotherly loyalty.

A nice feature of Little League and PONY League was the fact that the coaches had us playing different positions. Coming up in the ranks, I had the chance to play the outfield, first base, and pitch. Since I was left-handed, my positions were based on where a left-handed player fit into the structure of the diamond. The rule is that first basemen should be left-handed and shortstops should be right-handed. This is because of the crossover effect that occurs during the course of making plays. Conventional wisdom says that a left-handed shortstop and a right-handed first baseman would be pivoting the whole game—which might slow or hurt the team.

So, as a lefty, I was destined *not* to play shortstop. Except for one thing, one minor detail, everything was settled: I *knew* I could play shortstop, and I was bent on proving it to Dad.

I had been bugging him to give me a shot when, as it happened, our regular shortstop was injured just before an important game. What better chance to let me play that position the way I knew I could play it?

Dad said no.

Beside myself, I cried nonstop before the game trying to get him to change his mind. Nothing would move him. I couldn't understand his reasoning for the life of me.

But Dad stuck to his baseball knowledge and his decision based on what was best for the team. He was not about to let some crying kid, even if it was his own son, dictate protocol on the diamond. I took ground balls all morning long, even in our own front yard before we left! In the game I hit a home run, and it was all worth it. Fortunately, I learned a lesson about respecting the decisions of management, even when I disagreed—an experience that served me well down the line.

Robert was just as intense about baseball as I was. A notable display of his intensity happened during a close championship game in 1973 that we played against the Worthington Cardinals when my father waved Robert to third base on a single hit by me. Unfortunately, he might have overestimated Robert's being able to make it to third base that day. The umpire called Robert out, but then he saw that the third baseman had missed the tag and that Robert was really safe. So he changed his call to safe.

We were thrilled, except that Coach Chick had never called time-out. He was not about to argue, but Robert was in the face of the umpire, unaware of the safe call. The third baseman, aware that the call was changed to safe, then tagged the arguing Robert out with his glove.

Now called out, and blaming Dad, Robert stormed back to the dugout cussing at Dad and going nuts. This was bad sportsmanship to the nth degree, and Dad, making sure Robert knew he'd crossed the line, threw him into the dugout.

"Chick, are you crazy!" yelled Mom, leaping up from her aluminum lawn chair in disbelief.

Robert had learned the tough lesson that you can take losses badly, but you can't cross the line and yell at other people. Dad's attitude was that it was acceptable to be hard on yourself, to a point, but it was not okay to be hard on others around you. It corrupted the "team" concept.

My brother Kevin, who had the athletic gift of great speed in the family, took being hard on himself too far when he once viciously slapped himself after losing a one-on-one basketball match.

Dad, who was always watching from the porch, yelled, "Kev, what the heck is wrong with you?" That pretty much put an end to senseless displays of bad behavior of that sort.

How not to be hard on myself was a mystery that dogged me for years. Many batting helmets and watercoolers would tell those tales later on.

But being a midwesterner and an O'Neill, I wore the game on my sleeve and couldn't for the life of me understand how a person strikes out and likes it. I loved the game, and I hated to lose. Sometimes this idea of love of the game just transformed itself into something explosive. In retrospect I wouldn't have changed a thing, because I'm not the type of person who can strike out with the bases loaded and laugh about it. I carry failure around with me for a while.

Dad tried to help me put my focus on learning from mistakes. On the other hand, he was ultimately more concerned about allowing me and my siblings to find our own ways, whether it was in baseball or in life. He wanted whatever love my brothers and I would have for the game of baseball to come from within us, not because of pressure from him.

His emphasis was just on enjoying the experience of playing base-ball. I'll always remember the smile on his face at the Dairy Queen after an intense game well won. Even if we didn't win, the shakes tasted just as great, and his smile was just as big.

Dad was the definitive motivator who accentuated the positive. If I was beating myself up about a ground ball I could have caught that hopped right past me on the pitcher's mound, he'd switch the subject to tell me that my line drive in the fourth inning was great.

"You'll go get 'em tomorrow," he'd tell me, his familiar refrain when we'd lose.

"I didn't hit a home run," I'd mope.

"But you hit the ball right on the button, son!" he'd insist, getting in the last word.

This was our running bit, phrases I heard repeated often but that usually worked at cheering me up.

Sometimes he used the parental technique of trying to distract me. There was one loss I remember that came after Dad hadn't pitched me for one straight week to save me for a big upcoming doubleheader. I pitched nine innings that day and woke up with a stiff neck. By the next game, I couldn't throw, and we ended up losing. Dad tried consoling me, but all I wanted to do was pout, although he did convince me to go to the movies that night. The one playing happened to be *Jaws*. Thank God for that movie, because instead of focusing on having gotten killed on the baseball field, I was too busy concentrating on that shark and who *it* was going to kill!

On several occasions we faced the Pierce Brothers team, sponsored by a dry-cleaning company. After a long game that I pitched against them, giving it everything I had, we were beaten 1–0, a complete-game loss. Afterward I wasn't merely upset—the heartbreaker had me in utter shambles.

Dad came over to quietly console me. "Paul, you pitched a great game," he insisted.

There was no talking to me. Who cared how well a person did if he was the losing pitcher? I was the one with the loss on my record, the reason the team had lost the game. I felt personally defeated. All I wanted was to have that game back to win.

In those moments Dad's praise for the good points of what I'd accomplished fell on deaf ears. Only much later did I get it. He was proud of me, regardless of the loss. He was proud of my talent and proud of my effort. And that was really what winning was about after all, my desire to make my father proud.

The Julian Speer A's, as our Little League team was known, since that was the construction company that sponsored us and because a lot of us were Oakland Athletics fans, earned a following. Decked out in the A's colors, I thought we were the coolest in our white cleats and the green-and-gold jersey shirts. My brothers also loved the A's and watching Reggie Jackson play in that 1970s A's dynasty team.

Following baseball on television offered our household more opportunities for camaraderie and excitement. The All-Star Games were events I geared up for a week early. I saw every pitch, right there on my color television—which was another big treat, watching baseball in color. One of the most unforgettable All-Star Games that we watched was the one at Tiger Stadium when Reggie slugged that monster home run in right field that hit the top of the roof and bounced off the light standards. Also memorable was the All-Star Game with the Fred Lynn grand slam, as well as the game when Dave Parker made an unbelievable throw from the outfield. Even as a kid, I loved to watch the outfielders throw runners out at home with a cannon shot.

Sometimes I'd succeed in making plays of my own sort of like that, especially in the Plain City Tournaments where our Little League seasons culminated. Plain City is a small Amish community outside the city of Columbus, a rustic town where life is simple and the folks are devoted to God in their pious customs and ways.

The ballpark itself was an experience, a majestic oasis in Plain City where we played at night under the lights, the baseball field manicured to the hilt. It was beautiful. Instead of lines or makeshift barricades, the ballpark had a real fence to aim for, and for us to play in a park where we had the possibility of hitting home runs over a real fence made us feel that we were playing in the major leagues. There was a concession stand, an announcer, and a scoreboard, none of which we had in most other area ballparks.

When a tournament game arrived, Dad loaded us into the back of his Ranchero, the eight of us dressed in our uniforms, cleats on and all, and drove us the forty-five-minute ride there from Columbus. Our ritual was to bring along big packs of chewing gum and stick as many wads of gum into our mouths as we could. What else could a kid want? We felt like major-leaguers and carried ourselves that way. I'll never forget those rides home in the dark with the country air down the long, rural roads into the city.

Winning the tournament in 1973 meant as much to me at that point in my life as the World Series meant two decades later! I was ten years old playing in a league of twelve-year-olds—a feat in itself—and that year, 1973, I hit .400. Hitting for average! Dad was right. As a ten-year-old in that league, or at any age, that was huge. I was on top of the world.

Life couldn't have been any better. The chocolate milk shake at the Dairy Queen was the icing on the cake.

Two years later I pitched, and we won the Plain City Tournament when I struck out Darren Wall, a tough little left-handed hitter, on a 3–2 curveball. I'll never forget that strikeout as long as I live. How could I? The smile on Dad's face was emblazoned forever in my heart. Plain City was our World Series.

———— • ————

THREE

Team O'Neill

Winter in Columbus, Ohio, brought snowstorms so blinding there were nights when I couldn't see out the windows. Even when I was a teenager, these times were worrying to me because of the many nights Dad wasn't home with us but was out doing an all-night plowing shift so he'd have some extra time and money for us. That way, because construction was slow, he could make ends meet and still afford time in his schedule to be able to cheer us on in our deep-winter high-school basketball games that he hated to miss.

Dad's Nebraska upbringing and his war experience had weathered him to be able to handle snowplow shifts that might last twenty-four hours straight. Often, while I was still snug asleep in my bed, he was out clearing roads, driveways, and parking lots before the crack of dawn so people could drive to work, then going wherever he was called throughout the day and into the night again. What worried me was remembering the one night when I was fourteen and Mom broke the news to me that Dad had been in an accident. He had fallen off the machine and was almost unconscious in the parking lot because he had pushed himself too far.

That was one of the few times when I was growing up that it occurred to me that Dad was actually human. No matter how fearless and truly courageous he was—standing up to the forces of nature in daily life—he was still vulnerable to the elements. Despite his herculean abilities, his athletic background, and his natural strength with those big, powerful hands of his, he still needed to eat and sleep. Clearly, a person could only go so long without collapsing. He pushed himself to his limits for us, and I often asked myself, What would drive someone to push himself that hard? The answer was always the same: Dad loved his family.

While it scared me to imagine what it must have been like for him to be alone and helpless, suddenly collapsing outside in the freezing cold, it also inspired me as an example of what fatherhood and husbandhood were all about. The fact that he didn't stop pushing snow after that experience, but got right back out there when he recovered, showed me something Dad tried to teach in other ways as well—that in life you sometimes have to roll with the punches. That was my father's knack, his left-handed, one-of-a-kind way of doing things.

Whether he consciously intended it or not, Dad was giving me a blueprint for living.

As long as there were no blinding snowstorms, winter brought the joys of ice-hockey season—during which my brothers and I spent every spare moment glued to our backyard rink. We made it ourselves by damming up the pond, flooding it with water, and allowing it to freeze over. On those occasions when it snowed and we couldn't play, Dad would always come to the rescue, walking a couple of hundred feet to have the backhoe belch out its black smoke so he could use it to clear the rink for us to play. A wave of the hand and we were all ready to face off.

For years I made my own hockey sticks, starting back when I was nine and didn't have one of my own. With plywood I got from Dad, I used a jigsaw to carve out the frame. Then, using black electrical tape, I taped the blade and finished up spray-painting the stick with metallic copper paint. Presto—a cool black-and-copper hockey stick. Who needed to go to the sporting-goods store and slap down real money for a brand-name piece of equipment when you could make it yourself? Those homemade sticks lasted for years.

Dad's resourcefulness rubbed off on all of us. We used whatever we had—brooms, store-bought hockey sticks, homemade sticks of various kinds, even ones made from tomato stakes. Baseball catcher's gear was recycled for goalie pads, and a shuffleboard puck was transformed into an ice puck. We had it all—rink, sticks, puck, goalies, and players.

In typical O'Neill brotherly fashion, the competition was fierce. Once during a game, my brother Kevin knocked into me so hard that he threw me off my skates and over a fence. Pat—about Dad's height and build, with a powerful barrel chest—was my teammate in that game, and he quickly roughed up Kevin as payback. What was hockey without a little unnecessary roughness?

We lit bonfires in an open spot on the property to accompany the games, which added another dimension of fun to the festivities. In junior high and high school, when there weren't basketball games scheduled, an informal get-together with brothers, friends, and neighbors for some hockey also brought out some of our girlfriends, who stayed warm around the fire until we joined them after the game.

One winter night we had a minor crisis when it was our neighbor Bruce Schaefer's turn to chip in the firewood. Seeing as his dad was out of town and their stock of firewood was gone, we all went ahead and took most of the tomato stakes from the Schaefers' backyard and used them for the bonfire.

When Mr. Schaefer came back from vacation and didn't say anything, we thought nothing of it. In the springtime, however, he stopped by to let us know about all his missing tomato stakes. "Boy," he said, shaking his head, "those termites are really bad this year!"

You can imagine how hard it was to keep our faces straight with that remark.

My brothers may not have known how much I idolized them and to what extent they influenced me. To me they were the coolest in every respect—their humor and mischief-making, their hip 1970s hairstyles and clothing, their athletic abilities, and especially their taste in music. Because of what they played most of the time, my musical idols followed suit, with the likes of the classic rock and rollers such as The Rolling Stones, Led Zeppelin, and Neil Young's bands—including Crosby, Stills, Nash & Young—along with many of the Motown artists.

My brothers and I took turns cranking up the music and blasting it throughout the house with these big tall speakers—so loud I could feel my chest vibrating with the music.

Since Mom was adamant that, aside from all the sports, we incorporate some form of educational extracurricular activity into our schedule, my choice was to take drum lessons. In my extracurricular fantasy, I was every legendary rock drummer, although my main dreams continued to be about baseball.

One scenario I dreamed up was about being the outfielder and making a bang-bang play at the plate. I could visualize it in thrilling detail: Just as a vicious line-drive single is hit to me, a runner on second tears off and rounds third base, wanting to test my arm. Catching the ball—

bang!—I throw a cannon to home plate, and—bang!—the ump yells at the runner, "Yer out!" Play over. Dream over.

And yet I wanted this dream to come true. I wasn't scared of it. I wanted the ball. Dad had brought me to a place in my baseball education where I was never scared of being at the center of a crucial play. Why be scared? After all, like he said, if things went wrong, then I'd just go out and get 'em tomorrow.

The player who probably most qualifies as my true childhood idol and who inspired me throughout my career was Willie Mays. Willie played from the early 1950s to the early 1970s, and his athleticism and the joy he had for the game were incomparable. In the five different categories of baseball skills—from hitting, hitting for power, running, fielding, and throwing—Willie Mays was great in every area. I admired him for his flair as a player and for his grace in the outfield. He made impossible catches and throws look effortless. He was fast on the base paths, ran his heart out, and was a home-run hitter who hit over .300 year after year. To be an all-around, consummate player like Willie— that was the dream.

Needless to say, baseball heroes had to include the legends of the Big Red Machine era—Joe Morgan, Johnny Bench, and Pete Rose— that I'd been lucky to watch in my early years. They were *my* Cincinnati Reds.

To this day I can remember a game from thirty years ago, seeing Joe Morgan at second base, Pete Rose sliding hard into third with the dust swirling in the air. On defense there was Don Gullett on the mound and Johnny Bench behind the plate. Over the years my brothers and friends and I saved Big Red baseball cards and pined to get their autographs on a given summer's night at Crosley Field. What I would have given to play on a team with Pete Rose or to throw a ball to Johnny

Bench. I would have loved some fielding instruction from the great Joe Morgan on how to go left and then pivot ever so perfectly and throw that runner out at first base.

Then I would wonder, if I ever did make it, would fans care about me as much as I cared about my childhood idols?

Then again, my greatest baseball idols always cared the most about me. They were my own father and brothers.

Mom and Dad were a team, always a team the two of them, co-captains of the larger team that included my sister, my brothers, and me. Winter, spring, summer, fall—in every season my parents were involved in our lives. When I went on to play PONY league and high-school baseball and Dad wasn't coaching one of our teams, he and Mom drove us to the park and the two sat together in the stands—cheering me on.

Whenever I stepped off the pitcher's mound, I could see them applauding. Two sunburned people just smiling from ear to ear watching me play.

My parents cheered us all and had confidence in all their children's abilities. Robert, for instance, was amazing in his junior-high basketball games. There was one away game, at Linmoor Junior High, that Dad and I went to watch in which Robert's team was down to the final thirty seconds and the coach, playing it safe, told him to hold on to the ball. My brother had different plans, however. He took a quick shot and nailed it! Robert won it for the team! The place went nuts. Fights broke out in the stands and, since we were the enemy, Dad and I knew we had to get out of there as quickly as possible.

The two of us ran to the parking lot at top speed, racing each other to the car, just as one of the disgruntled fans of the opposing team careened in my direction, hauled off, and punched me right in the face—in broad daylight. I went down, got up, leaped into the car, and Dad hurried us out of there, getting us home in one piece.

If junior-high fans could get that rough, what did that tell me about fans at the higher levels? As much as Dad had talked about sportsman-ship on and off the field and the court, my conclusion was to avoid stooping to that level, to stay above the fray.

For the most part, I was able to do just that, although that occasion would not be the last time I witnessed fights erupting after basketball games.

My years at Brookhaven High School were everything I could have wanted and more. The *best*. Even the walk to school—through our front yard, then through another front yard, then a backyard and a jump over a fence before putting me on the high-school grounds—was out of a storybook. Coming home for lunch was no problem either.

What I loved was that high school offered me a time to explore all kinds of academic subjects and sports before I really had to make a decision about my future. The structure allowed me to be myself, and I flourished in several areas. By now, at my full height of six-four, I was tall, a trait that came from Mom's side of the family, and besides base-ball, I was enjoying playing football and basketball—the latter so much so that I thought about going to college to play basketball.

As a freshman I was lucky enough to play football as the starting quarterback. My friend Bobby Moore was one of the fastest guys around, and we always practiced long passes together, eager to make some big plays on game days. Sure enough, there was one spectacular game in which I threw him a monster pass and he suddenly became a

TV sports highlight film unto himself—jumping up and catching the ball in midair and bringing it down in the end zone to score the game-winning touchdown.

We were big men on campus at the postgame party. We were fifteen years old, and this life seemed pretty perfect—a touchdown and then a big party.

Football took a backseat to basketball because the seasons conflicted, and so my quarterbacking days came to an end. Fortunately, I had some proud freshman-year football memories that I carried with me from then on. In the meantime, however, at least during the winter months, basketball was my sport.

It might have made a slight difference that there was a certain beautiful cheerleader on the basketball cheering squad named Nevalee Davis.

During our childhood, into junior high, and then high school, at every turn, somehow Nevalee was always there, her path crossing mine. A friendship that had started at age five had eventually become romantic in high school—like a movie. As a matter of fact, on one of our first dates we went to the drive-in to see *Grease*—my favorite movie of all time. Even though this was the late 1970s, I related so much to a movie about those all-American bobby-sox days, an era that had a lot in common with the midwestern hometown upbringing I had in Columbus, Ohio. It was also romantic—John Travolta and Olivia Newton-John were classic young lovers.

We both loved *Grease,* but we had different tastes in music. Because Nevalee's older brothers and sisters were out of the house already, she had been raised much like an only child—not exposed to some of the sixties stuff that I was by my siblings. The music I loved was hard-core rock, compared to her preference for Top 40 and popular hits from the radio. At visits to my house, her eyebrows were just a bit raised. I imagined her wondering, *What are these guys into? What's going on here? Who are the Who, the Allman Brothers, the Doors?*

But for all our differences, we balanced each other out in many ways.

In high school, having a girlfriend as a cheerleader for our basketball team made me feel she was cheering and doing her jumps *for me.*

Our basketball team was really top-notch. One game that stands out was against our rivals, Linden-McKinley, whose coach, Gene Davis, had made them a powerhouse, leading them to the State AAA championships two times—a high-school basketball dynasty. Jimmy Cleamons, a Cleveland Cavs guard, and boxer Buster Douglas had played for them. Then they suffered a crushing loss in double overtime as they tried to in-bound the ball and *I* stole it! I took off, running full court, and dunked for a Brookhaven victory. The place went nuts, with fist-fights in the bleachers. Before we knew how bad it was, the police showed up and had to come down to the floor to usher us into the locker room for our protection. Just before we left the court, I turned back and saw my brother Mike get punched. The pugilist of the family, at six foot four Mike isn't the type of guy you want to get mad. Without hesitating, he punched the guy right back, sending him through a door. Taking no prisoners as usual, Mike upheld the family name, for sure.

For all the thrills I got from the nonstop, heart-racing rhythm of basketball—those postgame fights notwithstanding—baseball continued to be my true love.

Junior year I had an early taste of local baseball celebrity when my picture appeared in the paper after we won the city championships and I pitched a no-hitter. Winning was a dream come true in itself, not to mention that it was against one of our rival schools—Eastmoor High School. Archie Griffin, the only two-time Heisman Trophy winner, and his brother, Ray, also an NFL player, played there. Being a hero was a great feeling, but so was cheering on my teammate and best friend,

Cecil Howell, who won an earlier tight tournament with his biggest rival, Northland High School, by hitting a clutch home run and helping his school win the city championships.

These victories delighted Dad to no end. He loved seeing me following in his footsteps on the pitcher's mound all through high school, although he seemed to take some of his greatest pleasure in watching me hit line drives.

Knowing that I was starting to feel torn about which sport—basketball or baseball—would be my calling, Dad refrained from telling me what to do, wanting whatever decision I ultimately made to be my own.

By senior year, after I'd continued to pitch well, I heard the buzz that scouts for the pros were going to be coming by the baseball field to watch me pitch. I didn't know when, but I was informed that they were interested in me. Then my coach gave me a heads-up, letting me know the scouts were definitely going to be coming the next day. Aware that our team was planning an all-night party at a local bowling alley, my coach warned, "Don't stay out late. Don't bowl. Don't hurt that arm. Scouts will be in the stands tomorrow to watch you. Go home and get your rest."

Just as he had suggested, I dropped by the bowling alley, stayed only a little while, didn't bowl, and went home to get my rest, psyching myself up for the scouts. Proud of having done the right thing, I figured my reward would be in the form of a big win the next day and a dazzling display for the scouts.

The next day came after an anxious night's sleep. As promised, there they were in the stands—radar guns, clipboards, and straw hats. They looked liked scouts and acted like scouts, all packed together in one section, sticking out like sore thumbs.

With great composure I strode out to the mound, grabbed the rosin bag, and went to work. Pitch after pitch, hit after hit. The first inning I got absolutely drilled. I gave up six runs, all earned, in that one inning and had to be taken out of the game! It was a disaster. Unbelievable. All these runs were stuck on the scoreboard in less than one inning of work. I was dying inside as I walked off the pitcher's mound, and it was hard to miss seeing that the scouts were packing up their bags like a horde of ants ready to desert the colony.

Head down, thoroughly dejected, I made my way to the dugout, thinking I should have just bowled and had a good time last night. They were never coming back, I was sure. I honestly believed I had blown any chance I might have had to be scouted for professional baseball.

My dad, as always the ultimate optimist, had a different view. "They'll come back," he assured me.

Dad was right, the scouts did come back. Next time they apparently liked what they saw, and word trickled back to me that everyone was pretty high on me. That changed everything.

Now, nearing graduation, I had two pivotal decisions to make. First, was it going to be basketball or baseball? And second, would I go to college and play one of those two sports or begin my professional sports career right out of high school?

The first decision was the easier. In all honesty, I had already made up my mind by this time. The answer was in my blood. It had to be baseball.

The second decision—going to college or not going—was agonizing, so much so that most of the college recruiting letters I received remained unopened in a brown grocery bag. Gene Bennett, a scout for the Cincinnati Reds, was hoping to persuade me to sign right out of high school and go to their Montana farm club. He said I'd be an outfielder for the club, not a pitcher, if I decided on the route of going straight to the minors and not going to college.

Dad was 100 percent in favor of the move from pitcher to outfielder.

But as to whether I should sign immediately or get a college education, he said, "Paul, that's your decision. It's up to you." He counseled me to look within myself and choose what I really wanted out of life.

In one direction was the dream of playing professional ball, nurtured my whole life, which now had a real chance of coming true. Not in the future, but now. In the other direction was the path of college, which was important to my family.

At the same time, if I went to college it would be to play baseball. Bottom line, that was what I really wanted to do in life. At long last, after much soul-searching, I decided that deferring the dream was not for me. My thinking was, *Let's get this over with right now and go play ball*.

Making the decision was hard enough, but breaking it to Mom was probably even tougher. Pass up going to college? With her own degree and educational training, not only did she want us to have the opportunities in life that education can bring, but she had never seen baseball as a real career for me—or anyone else for that matter.

There was no question that she had loved seeing me play the game, that she had been in my cheering section throughout my youth, and that she recognized I was talented. But baseball as a job? The concept of being able to make money and support myself playing a game was understandably alien to her. Still, she set her reservations aside and joined with Dad and the rest of my family to wish me victory in my quest.

If some of Mom's well-founded fears for me had been realized, if my dream of playing baseball had not come true, I'm not sure what I would have done instead. Probably I would have ended up working in the family construction business. But the idea that I wasn't going to be playing baseball never entered my mind. Dad had taught me that hope springs eternal, that if I set my mind to doing something, I'd achieve it—as long as I was good enough and gave it my very all.

When I looked back over the foundation I'd been given—the place and the times that bred me, the natural abilities God had given me, the girlfriend who loved me, and the sister and brothers, mother and father who taught and inspired me—it seemed that I had something else important going for me: I was pretty darn lucky.

PART

II

1981–1992

FOUR

Road to the Majors

T he journey to the majors on which I set out in the summer of 1981 at age eighteen would prove to be much longer and more winding than the straight shot to the big time that I'd first expected.

I came to understand what Dad had often said in the past—that baseball is a marathon, not a sprint. This popular truism puts each game, and each season, and an entire career, into perspective. And yet for a rookie in the minor leagues, at least for me, learning this came as something of a rude awakening. I found myself trying to apply what Dad had emphasized to me through the years—that if a player just thinks of each game and each season as part of one long, unfolding season, a slow, steady climb to the top, the player will do fine. The challenge was to make every moment and every step count, even when the greater goal seemed out of sight. Dad always told me that there was no such thing as doing too much—not only in the big games but also early in the season and even in practice.

Whether I was up to that test, my minor-league journey was about to reveal.

It didn't take long to figure out that all those glimpses on television and in the movies that showed the lifestyle of a major-league player bore little resemblance to what I was encountering. As it turned out, the minor-league life, as opposed to the major-league life, was not dawn versus dusk. It was night versus day.

Of course, I was like everyone else on draft day, thinking I'd make it to the majors in all of three weeks. The myth of overnight stardom is as false in professional sports as it is in show business. The truth is that behind almost every new young sensation is a story of hard work, dedication, and perseverance in the face of disappointments. The cold baseball reality is that most players drafted at eighteen won't make the major leagues for four or five years. That is, if they make the majors at all.

But if I had been presented with that realistic scenario, I wouldn't have believed it. Being a fourth-round draft pick by the Reds, basically my hometown team—as a teenager right out of high school—was simply too much of a dream come true. And so, with the Reds' decision to send me to start with their club in Billings, Montana, I left home just two days after graduation from Brookhaven High School, bags packed and new dreams in tow.

No sooner had I set my suitcases down in my small room at the Northern Hotel in Billings, than some of the bubbles began to burst. It suddenly occurred to me that, for the first time in my life after growing up in our unique bustling family atmosphere, I was *alone*. Out here in Big Sky country, the scenery was gorgeous, but, compared to the fairly cosmopolitan city of Columbus, Billings was pretty much out in the middle of nowhere—not exactly a stone's throw from home.

During the hours that I was busy getting to know the rest of the

Billings Mustangs and actually playing baseball, I managed to keep my spirits up. But the moment I returned to the hotel, I became a nervous wreck. All of a sudden, the mystique of my family baseball lineage wore off really fast. Pro baseball player or not, I was a scared kid just out of high school, on my own with nobody around, hundreds of miles from family and friends, homesick, and worried as to whether I'd chosen the right career path in life.

Within that first week, my bright future began to appear bleak.

Then I heard that there were local families renting out rooms and taking in some of the players. Initially I was too shy to say anything, but, with the way I wanted out of my lonely hotel room, I piped up and asked the team management if there were any openings left. The answer came back that a family named the Broeders had enjoyed the experience of taking in a hockey player before and were open to the idea of having me stay with them.

Blessings come in all sorts of ways, and the Broeders—Linda and Gary and their two kids, Eric and Kristen—were true godsends.

After the arrangements were made and a very reasonable rent was set, they picked me up as planned and welcomed me into their home. But then, after a week of making me feel like one of the family—with my own room, Linda's home cooking and cleaning on my behalf—they announced that they wouldn't accept any money from me! I couldn't believe it. They were amazing. Their lives revolved around my schedule, and they couldn't do enough for me. Gary even let me drive their VW Bug whenever I needed a car to get around on my own.

The Broeders became my surrogate family while I was away from home for those three months of the season following the June draft, and they were responsible for helping make my first year in the minor leagues a fun adventure—very different from the lonesome and disappointing way it started. We have stayed in touch ever since those days, and they were able to come visit in Seattle and Kansas City when I happened to be playing in those cities later on.

Just how lucky I was became evident when I saw that many of the younger players who weren't taken in by families seemed not to fare as well in the minors as those who were. A large part of being able to make the transition to the minors, I learned, was not just handling what happened between the foul lines, but handling the curveballs thrown our way outside the lines.

Another helpful factor was that, in general, professional baseball players are placed on a pedestal, even in the minor leagues. The fans who turn out game after game to watch their teams play in the minor-league contests are indeed a breed of their own, devoted and true baseball lovers. Traveling to different towns and cities and playing to stands full of strangers, it was humbling to go to the plate and hear the crowd express enthusiasm at the announcement of my name, some even starting to follow my career. This was important to me, as it is for everyone who comes up through the ranks. Every ballplayer at every level, no matter what he might tell you, needs and thrives on fan approval. As a homesick kid, playing in ballparks where I didn't know anyone, I really appreciated those crowds who made me feel at home.

In Billings the small community really rallied around the Mustangs, cheering us on as athletes and as local celebrities. That support reminded me how fortunate I was to be living my dream, and it definitely helped me in the long haul.

Daily practice was from nine to five. Another drastic change from high school.

Much of the time spent between practice and games was on buses—trips that sports announcer Michael Kay (a close friend of mine later in my Yankees era) might have called "an unmanageable sixteen hours." After a game played at home one night, we had enough time to shower before leaving that same night on a bus trip to another minor-league park far away, a trip that lasted those sixteen unmanageable hours. At our destination I was so thankful just to be able to stand and walk off the bus, but as soon as we shook the creaks out and arrived in the visiting town, after an entire night of travel, it was time to play a game that same night. Often there was barely enough time to get to the ballpark.

Hopscotching across the country, in between games and practice, I telephoned home like crazy, more than anyone else on the team. During the first summer away, whenever I called all my friends, they gave me news of how much they were enjoying their summers and looking forward to getting ready to head off to college. A nagging voice inside wondered if that wasn't where I should be, if giving up that chance was going to be worth it. They talked about subjects they'd be taking that fall semester, and I spoke about the previous night's ball game. How different our back-and-forth conversations seemed from weeks before when we were living the same life.

The contrast was hard to shrug off. The fact that they were moving toward the same future in school together, as a large familiar group, and I was headed in a totally different direction, a tenuous direction, was what weighed on my mind more than anything.

There were no guarantees for me. I was making six hundred dollars a month. The routine brought no other frills. This was it—what you see is what you get—for six months. If I didn't make it and get called up, the years would just be lost and college would have passed me by, all for nothing.

Heavy as those thoughts were, without knowing it I was also developing a new toughness, as the sixteen-hour bus trips and the long days made me realize that there was a method to the madness. Teams have a farm system not only to foster talent but also, just as important, to weed out talent. They try to make sure that certain players make the majors, and they try to make sure that certain players go home crying, dejected, and wanting to never pick up a baseball again.

What I eventually came to believe is that teams don't draft young players to groom them and give them a helping hand up to the majors; instead they're really drafting young players with the intention of weeding them out at the minor-league level. It's a system in which only the strong survive.

What helped me to survive was the decision to use this time—a year's tenure at the most, I figured—to become the best ballplayer I could be and build on the foundation Dad had given me.

The decision to move me to right field was one of the best things to happen that first year in the minors. Playing in such a range of different ballparks, I tasked myself with trying to become familiar with the terrain of the various right fields, the play of the walls, and the caroms. Those are the trajectories, for want of a better phrase, in which the ball bounces off the walls. It was an education to see the subtleties in how ballparks play and how the walls in some parks don't give the same caroms as do the walls in other parks.

As for what I did at bat, as Dad had always said, I worked for hitting right on the button and finished the 1981 season in Billings with a .315 batting average, 3 home runs, 29 RBIs, and 6 stolen bases.

Dad had taught me well.

By the end of 1982, I had moved up in the minors to the Reds' Cedar Rapids club, but now that I'd been playing just over a year, there was still no sign of the imminent jump to the majors I'd expected by this time.

During the off-season it had been comforting to be with family and to see a few friends, although most of them were away at college by the time I arrived home that fall. There was a widening gulf between their world and mine.

Back on the long bus trips, still calling home more than anyone else, I did enjoy the baseball I played that season, especially during the visits from Dad—who stayed true to his word, as he did every season, to travel as much as he could to watch me play. A highlight for us both when I was in AA ball that year was his coming all the way to Buffalo to see me play, as it so happened, in the ballpark that provided the backdrop for the great baseball movie *The Natural*, with Robert Redford.

For the 1982 season, I hit .272, but I had 8 home runs, 71 RBIs, and 12 stolen bases. Once more I inched upward and was moved to the Tampa club for the 1983 season.

In Florida I had my first serious thoughts about giving up. Money was so scarce, I wasn't even making long-distance telephone calls. To make everything worse, I was in a real batting slump. It was a slump like none I had ever experienced, a seemingly never-ending slump.

My dad's theory on slumps was that a player comes out of them when he can mentally move on to the next at-bat. I knew that my father was right. From early on, he had stressed his belief that a great part of being successful at playing professional baseball entails being able to fail and keep on moving. His tried-and-true secret to success—"Just go get 'em the next day"—was what I needed to embrace. If I couldn't fail and move on, I'd take every previous at-bat with me into my next at-bat, and that would just compound the problem.

But throughout the steamy Tampa season and stifling bus rides I couldn't get the monkey off my back. Nothing worked. I really wanted to quit, to pack it all up and head home, and I was on the verge of doing just that.

And then, at my lowest low, an envelope arrived in the mail, addressed to me in my father's handwriting. As I sat down to read it, I unfolded a long letter that he'd written by hand on lined yellow paper. This was one of the few times Dad had ever put his feelings to paper for me. He recounted our family history, how his father had played in the minors and his uncle had played in the Pioneer League, and how he himself had played baseball. Reading his words off the page, it was almost as if he was physically there putting his arm around me, energizing me with the will to carry on, continuing with his pep talk about how I was *his* son and I was *not* going to quit and how I was *never* going to quit.

When I put the letter away, a subtle shift had taken place inside, giving me a sense of certainty that this was not the end of my baseball ride. I resolved to give it one more go, for the sake of myself and for the family. That letter propelled me to end up breaking out of my slump and racking up 51 RBIs and 20 stolen bases.

Dad had come to the rescue.

As before, he continued to visit as much as possible. He had an unlimited capacity for loving baseball. During minor-league training camp, after he finished watching me and my team practice, he loved sitting in the stands all day and watching other teams practice—not even knowing any of the players involved. His passion for the game ran that deep.

When he came to see my games and I was at a lunch break, instead of joining me, if there was another game taking place on the field, Dad would sit and watch that game. When I say he loved baseball, I'm not exaggerating.

I finished that year in Waterbury, Connecticut, coming away this time with 6 RBIs in fourteen games.

My spirits had definitely rebounded, powering me through the 1984 season in Vermont, where I finished the season with 16 home runs, 76 RBIs, and 29 stolen bases.

To supplement my small salary, in the off-season I worked for a sporting-goods company and was fortunate to have the support of my family throughout those lean years. Although it didn't feel like a totally normal life yet, my convictions told me that good days were ahead of me, that I'd summoned the stuff I needed to withstand the storm and make it to the major leagues.

With growing optimism, at age twenty-one I made about the best decision of my life when Nevalee and I were married. As I always tell everyone, "We grew up together, and then we grew together." I think that's why things were, and still are, so perfect between us. No one understood me better. I was like an open book to her.

The way I viewed marriage and being in the minors was that I needed the former to deal with the latter. Marriage gave me a sense of stability at a time in my life when my future seemed anything but stable. Nevalee's unconditional love was such that she was not only willing but wanted to be with me through the downs as well as the ups, through the least glamorous years. She and I were a team throughout the whole process up to the majors, and her parents, Pat and Forrest Davis, two of the most loving people on the planet, were an integral part of the extended support system that came from both sides of the family.

Nevalee's parents generously loaned us the use of their place in Florida for the winter months in the off-season—time to enjoy our newlywed status and an opportunity that allowed me to concentrate on training for the coming season.

My goal was to make 1985 the transformational year, and after I got word that I'd moved up to the top of the minors—the Triple-A Denver club—I saw an opportunity to make it happen. Everyone in both families was counting on me. Mentally and physically, I put the pedal down. It was do-or-die time.

At those moments when I succumbed to a wave of uncertainty, one of my main incentives for carrying on was the vision of having to tell my older brothers that I'd failed. Funny, but true. It was a throwback to my younger days, I guess. I couldn't stand to relive those memories of losing to them in basketball and hearing all about it at the dining room table—how I choked on the jump shot or at home-run derby, and how they outhit me.

Not much had changed. Part of the driving force behind why I put that pressure on myself is that I felt in my heart that I was playing to uphold the dignity of the O'Neill family name. To make my home team proud. Whenever I had a good game, I'd call and I'd let them know that I'd just hit a home run that night. Their vicarious pleasure in my success fueled me onward.

Everyone was out of the house for years by this time, but we were always in touch with one another by phone. Molly had her own career as a chef, which all started when she worked at Café at the Mews in Provincetown, on Cape Cod, and would later evolve into work as an accomplished food writer. My brothers, multitalented, were settling into businesses and successes of their own as well. My parents, who should have finally had some free time, helped support me, and the same went for Nevalee's parents.

Doing well was the least I could do in return for the belief everyone had in me.

Around this time I also received an important piece of good advice about my game from Gregg Riddoch, a man I deeply respected in the Reds organization who was considered to be the "pipeline to the majors." After watching me play during a couple of different visits, he pulled me aside and said something that woke me up.

"The only thing holding you back, Paul," he commented, "is your defense."

Those words made a ringing, and lasting, impression on me. From then on I worked feverishly to improve the part of my job that was played out in right field, taking pride in walking away with minimal errors.

Using every resource at my disposal, and most of all the determination to play to the best of my abilities in every aspect of the game, four years after high-school graduation, 1985 with the Denver club was my breakout year. I hit .305 for the season, led the league with 155 hits, led the league with 32 doubles, and had 74 RBIs. Right on the button.

And, fatefully, there I was in St. Louis on September 3, 1985, after being called up. A major-leaguer playing with the Cincinnati Reds, singling off the first pitch in my first game with them! All the hard work, all the determination, all the sweat and tears, all the combined dreams of loved ones—all worth it. A huge weight had been taken off of me. When I called Nevalee after talking to Dad and Mom, I tried to describe the feeling but couldn't find the words. It was like being on top of the world.

All I knew was, looking back from that place, I saw that everything had unfolded just as it was meant to, slump and all. And I decided that if I had it to do over again, the slow marathon run to this wonderful new beginning, I wouldn't have changed a thing.

What's more, I soon decided never to change the number that the Cincinnati Reds had assigned me for my debut major-league game— number 21. At the time it was a random occurrence, since that was a number that happened to be available. On the other hand, it felt lucky to me.

Even when I later had the choice to change, I continued to wear it—in honor of Roberto Clemente and his contributions to baseball.

In time number 21 was to become a part of me and who I was, what I expected of myself on the field when I played.

FIVE

My Cincinnati Days

SEPTEMBER 11, 1985, CINCINNATI'S RIVERFRONT STADIUM

Having only just arrived in the major leagues, I prepared to witness history unfold in front of my eyes from the best seat in the house—the dugout.

Millions across the country were watching, too, aware that Pete Rose was expected to break Ty Cobb's all-time major-league hit record of 4,191.

The day before had been a buildup to this moment, when the Reds played the Cubs at legendary Wrigley Field, in and of itself a thrill for me to play in that ballpark for the first time. Wrigley Field was everything that I'd heard about and seen from afar: the ivy-covered walls, the notorious "well" area that daunted the steeliest-nerved players, who would quake watching the ball hit—never knowing where and how fate would carry it off that wall.

By this era Wrigley Field was one of the last living dinosaurs of the old days before stadiums had lights. Later, in the 1990s, lights were finally installed at Wrigley Field—a loss for young people growing up today, because with the advent of the lights went a piece of baseball history. There is nothing like experiencing the excitement and tension of dusk falling during a climactic game.

Despite the lack of ballpark lights on the rainy afternoon of September 8, 1985, the place was nonetheless charged with a spine-tingling electricity. And when Pete Rose made his 4,191st hit to tie the record, the roar from the stands was deafening.

With the likelihood that Pete would break the record during his next at-bat, the anticipation intensified. The media and most of the public—including the die-hard Reds fans who had made the four-hour pilgrimage to Wrigley—were ecstatically geared up to see it broken that afternoon. But there were mixed feelings among Reds management and the millions of loyalists in Cincinnati watching on TV who really wanted to see Rose make his 4,192nd hit back home at Riverfront Stadium.

Somebody's prayers must have been heard. Just as the game was moving along, heavy rain set in. The game was called, and fate had Pete Rose going home for a date with destiny. Riverfront Stadium would host baseball history after all.

The next day came pretty fast for a wide-eyed guy like me, but it probably came way too fast for Pete. Then again, when you even mention his name, you think of only one phrase—the ultimate competitor. Throughout these events he handled everything in a way that only Pete could have.

Thus the stage was set. By game time the commissioner was on hand. The atmosphere was that of a playoff. The electricity of history in the air felt twice as intense as the day before.

Suddenly there was a cry from the umpire—*"Play ball!"*—and before I knew it, there I was, watching Pete Rose break Ty Cobb's all-time hit record from my dugout seat.

As soon as he reached first base, the bench emptied, and I was one of the players who tore onto the field to celebrate with Pete Rose, all of us surrounding him in jubilation. Pure euphoria! New to the major leagues, I felt like a kid back in Little League—jumping around, trying to get my face into the photo, in total disbelief that I'd be able to tell my friends and family that I saw Pete Rose break Ty Cobb's hit record right before my eyes.

That remains one of my top ten favorite big-league moments.

At this writing no one has yet to break Pete Rose's record set that very day. It will happen, though there are few individuals who have played this game that deserve to be mentioned in the same breath as Pete Rose. Legendary ballplayers like him will live on forever.

During my first two seasons with the Reds, Rose continued as a player/manager. It took me no time to realize that he managed with the same intensity with which he played, and he expected 100 percent from his players. Not necessarily great feats, but absolutely great effort.

Seasoned in the minors, I had no doubt in my mind that I was capable of great effort, wanting more than anything to prove myself worthy of staying with the Reds. I wanted to wear that uniform forever. I did *not* want to go back to the minors, not even for a second.

Even after I hit .333 for five games at the tail end of the '85 season, Rose didn't seem to know what to make of me and didn't play me very much through the '86 season, only three games—as if he were still trying to figure me out. Granted, I was not the everyday player, and I understood that this was a natural kind of feeling-out period.

After the '86 season, Pete Rose retired as a player yet continued as the Reds' manager. I knew that the next season, 1987, would be my make-or-break year. By this point Pete was ready to give me every opportunity to succeed, and I tried to make the best of each of them, ready to make the adjustments that would convince the Reds once and for all that I was to be a Cincinnati Red forever.

My chance came soon, as it had during my first game in the big leagues, when I entered a game as a pinch-hitter. The Reds were playing the Dodgers at Riverfront Stadium, with Kevin Gross pitching for the Dodgers. As I got into my left-handed batting stance, an old baseball expression came to mind: "See it, hit it."

I saw the pitch, timed it right, and knew with the crack of the bat against the ball that it was gone. I had hit a good shot out of the park for my first big-league home run.

Driving back to my house that night, I was in a kind of post-glory shock. Had that really happened? Did I really just hit a home run in the majors?

Dad's exuberant comment, after having seen it on TV, was voiced with fatherly confidence. "Just one of many to come," he knowingly predicted on the phone.

From his vantage point, my father saw the big picture as a sort of ledger sheet, believing that a player travels through his career in the major leagues filling up columns. There was the hit column, the home-run column, the stolen-base column, the RBI column, and the runs-scored column.

From my vantage point, in the smaller picture of surviving each hurdle, my concern was that the line between success and failure at the big-league level was so narrow it was hard to realize what was happening to you when you were in the moment. After the fact I often wondered what would have happened if I *hadn't* gotten that pinch-hit opportunity and *hadn't* hit that home run?

By this time my reputation for being hard on myself and for my level of passion was well established with my team. My teammate Lee May even went so far as to nickname me "Ordeal" because of the way I wore my heart on my sleeve.

Other players have different styles for taking things in stride when they don't live up to their own expectations. I could never take my hitting in stride, and I was equally obsessed about my defense.

Very prominent in my mind was the fact that just because I'd made it to the big leagues, that didn't mean I was immune from some of the challenges that had plagued me in the minors. And that included the one aspect of this game that really made me nuts—going through a slump.

The same slump that had haunted me and made me want to quit in the minors ate at my stomach in the majors. Slumps can make a ballplayer crazy, like a gambler on a losing streak who superstitiously believes that his luck has run out for good. It's a nightmare that makes you dread going to the ballpark. It gives you the jitters to get up to bat, because you don't know when this thing is going to end. Maybe it won't ever end, and you'll never get a hit again.

Dad knew how to nip those feelings in the bud and was there for me anytime. He didn't tell me to take it all in stride. He emphasized the affirmative, telling me positive things about my swing and stance and grip that had not entered my mind since the slump had set in.

As soon as I hung up the telephone, I wished I could be back in the batter's box that night, right then and there, at two o'clock in the morning. I wanted to face a pitcher, any pitcher, because I just knew that I could get a hit. The feeling usually carried over to the next day and enabled me to get back into my stride. Dad had the magic touch. Amazing.

Every game has its own music, its unique rhythm. Of course there's a set structure; the innings all have the same number of outs. Yet each game moves differently, its pace fast or slow, smooth and seamless, or stutter-stepping rock and roll.

My senses had become attuned to the rhythms as well as to the sounds of baseball, thanks to my father, who often observed the way different ballparks echoed the sounds of the game. His ear was so good that whenever a player cracked a good shot, Dad knew that it was gone before the announcers called it. Over the years he commented, for example, that the sound of Jose Canseco's bat was so loud it showed how powerful his wrists and forearms were, and it was no wonder why he hit those towering home runs. Glenn Braggs was someone who impressed my father on a pure strength level. This was a guy who could snap a bat like Bo Jackson, only Glenn did it on check swings. He was that strong. When, later on, Braggs was my teammate with the Reds, I used to feel sympathy with the pitcher on the visiting end of that line drive.

Looking back at individual games I can remember from Little League on, often the way I do so is by calling up their distinctive sounds and rhythms, as much as by recalling the play-by-plays. A very memorable Reds game against our rival Philadelphia Phillies was distinguished by the sound of laughter from my teammates, even though it was far from funny to me at the time.

The night started off innocently enough, and then suddenly, with the Phillies up to bat in the tenth inning, we were in jeopardy of losing the game.

Philadelphia's Steve Jeltz was the runner on second base, with Lenny Dykstra at the plate. John Franco was on the mound for us. The Reds' first baseman was Todd Benzinger. Out in right field, I was waiting to see what Lenny would do, an eye on Jeltz as well. If the ball was to me, I'd have one chance to make the play and get the ball home, or the game would be over.

After a tense exchange of signals, Franco readied with the windup and threw a fast pitch to Lenny, who saw it and hit a do-or-die shot to me. Ready, or so I thought, I reached for it and . . . I bobbled it! I didn't just bobble it—after it slipped from my glove the first time, I bobbled it again and dropped it! The ball rattled around my body, and, in my anguished frustration at having bobbled the play not once but twice, when it bounced toward my foot, all I could think to do was to kick that ball with all my might—right into the infield toward first base.

My baseball career flashed before my eyes. Promising future gone. Obviously we would lose the game, and it was entirely my fault. Visions of sixteen-hour bus rides clouded my brain. I was going back to the minors for sure. I couldn't believe it. They'd have me back in Nashville, reassigned to Triple-A minors, probably that same night.

But a split second later, when I blinked that vision away and turned my head toward third base, there was Steve Jeltz! What had happened? Why wasn't he in the dugout celebrating the Phillies' win?

Apparently what had happened was, because the turf was wet, Steve had slipped as he rounded third base, and the Phillies' third-base coach had held him up. He was unable to score as a result.

Lady Luck shone down on that game in more ways than one. Not only did Steve Jeltz slip, but miraculously, when I kicked the ball—instead of bouncing off into the stands, it went straight at first base.

The inning ended, but not as quickly as I would have liked. Back in the dugout, I sat down next to Todd Benzinger and held my head.

Benzinger gazed at me and thought for a minute. He had a reputation for looking like he was lost in his thoughts, wondering about esoteric subjects. Throughout our games he wore this ponderous expression all the time, so much so that the other guys and I often joked, asking each other, "What's Benz wondering about right now?"

Whatever it was, when I'd kicked the ball at him, between that and watching the runner, he was still puzzled enough to turn to me in the dugout and say, "You know, Paul, we would have had him at second base if you had just gotten something more on that throw."

My teammates were laughing hysterically. I was dumbfounded.

"Benz," I said, "I *kicked* the ball to you. Did you not see that I kicked the ball to you?"

Benz had no clue! He thought I'd thrown it. Ken Griffey Sr. and Lee May were hysterical, not sure what was funnier—the frustrated anguish of Ordeal (yours truly) or Benz's cluelessness.

After the laughter wound down, Pete Rose had every right to get in my face in the dugout, but he didn't. This was not his style of managing. When we made our next stop in New York to play the Mets, however, and I didn't play, I knew that he wasn't all too pleased with the bobbling and kicking maneuver in right field. He'd benched me, and he'd made his point.

Happily, I was back in for the next game and, trying to remember "just to go get 'em tomorrow," I found that I was able to laugh about the Phillies game.

As they say, all's well that ends well. By the end of the 1987 season, after 84 games as the Reds' top pinch-hitter, my performance had been strong and consistent.

Spring training in 1988 really felt like spring training, not like an audition. There was an energizing momentum building for the Reds, and it was a heady high to be a part of it.

Making it that much more meaningful was getting to look out to the stands and see Dad, totally enjoying himself as he soaked up every bit of this latest part of my baseball journey. Of all the road trips he made to see me play, being a part of spring training every year was *his* trip.

At first the Reds trained in Tampa, then moved their home site to Plant City. Each town had character to it and, wherever we were, Dad made the whole ambience of spring training even more fun. His presence certainly gave me tremendous confidence as I'd glance over and see him in the stands that held only around five thousand people, beaming at me with his constant big smile.

This was not a glamorous five-star vacation. In fact, we stayed in a modest rented apartment and spent long days at the ballpark. To Dad, who was in heaven watching me and the Reds practice, sitting in the sun all day long, hot dog in hand, talking it up with everyone around him, it was the vacation of his dreams. Every year I felt as if he were in his own training to get ready for the season.

Dad loved this annual trip so much he even cashed in bonds that were set aside to support him in retirement, just so that he could finance it! Just another one of his left-handed ways of doing things, as my brother Robert liked to point out.

Besides the input and advice my father continued to offer me, being in the company of my teammates, many of whom were famous veterans, provided me with an ongoing baseball education, and I was eager to learn all that I could from them.

Just as I had in the minor leagues, I made it my business to familiarize myself with the idiosyncrasies of terrain and caroms of the different big-league ballparks of all those National League teams we played.

One of the parks that really humbled me every time was Wrigley Field in Chicago. To play there is to play in an ivy-covered shrine. All of the stories of Cubs' announcer Harry Caray and players like Ernie Banks and Billy Williams brought out the ghosts of baseball past whenever we were there. For any outfielder the most humbling aspect of Wrigley Field comes when a ball gets snagged in the ivy that lines the outfield wall and the player has to struggle to fish it out—often to no avail. (Sammy Sosa today plays that right field wall with such perfection it amazes me.) For the right fielder, as I discovered, there is a further handicap—the angle of the sun. I was officially initiated into Wrigley outfield when the blinding sun made me lose the flight of the ball and, to make matters worse, its bounce took it deep into the ivy.

L.A.'s Dodger Stadium—with the white HOLLYWOOD sign perched in the hills to the west of it—was another park that made a player aware of baseball history, harking back to the days when Sandy Koufax rode the mound. With the movie industry all around, I could pick up a feeling of glamour and buzz, as show-business folks and devoted baseball fans mixed it up together.

It was against the Dodgers this year, on September 16, that I played in one of the three perfect games I've been fortunate to experience in my career, a chance few players get. It's hard enough to pitch a shutout—which means no runs are scored. Much harder still to pitch a no-hitter—which means opposing batters make no hits but may get on base by being walked or hit by a pitched ball. But pitching a perfect game—in which no opposing batter gets on base at all—is a once-in-several-lifetimes feat.

This was a clash of the Titans—when Reds' pitcher Tom Browning squared off against Dodgers' pitcher Tim Belcher. The game was a nail-biter all the way through the ninth inning, and Tom Browning would sail into baseball history. Belcher was equally amazing that day, matching Tom pitch for pitch. His stuff was also next to unhittable.

I didn't get a single hit off Belcher that game, although I did have a few hard line drives that found their way into the glove of Mike Marshall. I returned the favor by taking away a few potential hits from their players with some timely catches.

When it was over, Tom Browning had pitched a perfect no-hitter, sending twenty-seven Dodgers back to the dugout, winning the game for the Reds 1–0. This was the first perfect game in Cincinnati Reds pitching history.

With highlights like that, 1988 flew by, and in my first full-fledged, full-length season with the Reds, I came away with 16 home runs, 73 RBIs, and 8 stolen bases.

In the off-season, I decided to get myself into primo shape for the 1989 season and cranked up my workout with a weight-lifting and training program that included tennis as a new feature. Baseball players typically add a second sport, whether it's tennis or basketball, to make sure we keep our muscles lean and in tone and to help maintain flexibility.

My brother Robert, a fantastic tennis player who had been all-city in high school, had played with me sporadically over the years. As a baseball player, I couldn't play tennis in high school, since the schedules conflicted with each other, but I enjoyed the game, though not to the extent I did now that it was part of my workout regimen. A boost to my playing came when I met Steve Contardi, who ran a tennis club near us in Cincinnati and who's since become a good friend.

In traditional O'Neill form, I pursued my regimen with intensity— starting my day after rising early by lifting weights first thing in the morning, then lunch, and then tennis for the rest of the afternoon to loosen myself up. Lucky for me, star tennis player Jim Courier and I became friends in the process, since he was a baseball fan and particularly a Reds fan. I got him to some ballgames, and he played tennis with me.

Just watching Jim run across the court the first time, I sensed that, with his athletic instincts, if he hadn't been a tennis star, he'd have been an excellent baseball player. Shagging fly balls in the outfield, he had the innate knack for judging them well. Once the ball left the bat, he knew exactly where to position himself; they never went over his head, and he never took ridiculous leaps for them.

The one thing Jim wasn't game to do was to get into the cage. The risk of hurting his hand for tennis was too great. But he didn't have to prove anything to me. I was sure that if he ever did step inside that cage, he'd turn a few heads with some good rips.

My training in past seasons and in off-seasons paid off nicely in 1989, when I finished the year with an improved batting average, 15 home runs, 74 RBIs, and 20 stolen bases.

But my joy at the end of a terrific baseball season paled in comparison to the happiness that Nevalee and I, and our families, shared when—on September 30—our son Andrew was born.

Nothing had prepared me for the awe-inspiring wonder that came from being a parent.

Of course, gazing into Andy's eyes, I couldn't help feel that I was looking at the face of the next generation of O'Neill baseball players—no doubt the next right fielder in the family! And it wasn't really about raising him up Baseball, it was more about having someone to pass on all the life wisdom my dad had passed on to me.

Watching him grow and learn every day was incredible. Nevalee and I were head-over-heels in love with our baby boy.

This was beyond anything I could have dreamed. I had a little pal to play with and someone to call me Dad. "Papa Chuck," as he was to be known from now on in our household, now had a grandson from me, and he and my mom were tickled beyond words to have Andy to hold in their arms.

Children are truly the greatest blessings in our lives, bringing even more blessings with their arrivals.

Going into the 1990 season, a proud new father, I felt luckier than ever.

———— • ————

SIX

More Than Luck

After an off-season of changing diapers, giving late night feedings, and taking strolls around the house with Andy in my arms, it was suddenly mid-February again, time for me to head off to Florida for spring training.

By now the Reds had a formidable team, and I had never felt more confident in myself and in our chances for the 1990 season. The last few years of building for the future were over. The future was now.

The baseball world was beginning to take notice that Barry Larkin, Rob Dibble, and the rest of the Cincinnati Reds team had started to make a lot of noise in the National League. We were a solid team, both offensively and defensively. Barry Larkin was the team leader. His glove was amazing, and his offense was consistently above .300, the go-to guy who carried us when we needed the lift.

The only new factor in the mix for me was that Lou Piniella had come in to manage the Reds after the controversy that erupted over Pete Rose had caused him to be banned from baseball by the commissioner. Lou and I never had any overt problems, although in retrospect I could say that our respective emotional temperaments may have thrown off sparks when we didn't see eye to eye.

Lou could be abrasive. Say, for example, you were to ask him early on about weight training. He'd say that weight training to look good in a Polo shirt is fine, but that in baseball you can't be muscle bound. He was right to a degree, but his delivery could occasionally be less than friendly.

At times he was frustrated with me as a player because he thought I could do better, and I took that as a tremendous compliment. Lou was a great player and a great manager, and for him to *expect* more from me meant that he thought I had the ability to *do* more. Even back then, as a young player, I would rather have been seen as someone who could do better than someone in whom a manager had no faith because I lacked talent.

Despite those levels to our relationship, a feeling of mutual respect between Lou and me dominated for the roller coaster of a season the Reds were about to have.

This was the year that our team showed the city of Cincinnati a lot of heart. We came back in games we should have lost and won them in dramatic fashion.

Two of those games turned out to be two-homer games for me. The first was in Los Angeles against the Dodgers on June 2. The second came against the Giants on August 10 at Riverfront Stadium. In fact, 5 of the 16 homers I hit that year came off one pitcher—Don Robinson of the San Francisco Giants. In July I proved to be a nemesis once more when the Giants beat the Reds 4–0. In my last at-bat, just as Giants' pitcher Scott Garrelts was set to pitch a perfect game, with one out to go, I singled.

Whenever the Reds traveled to New York to play the Mets, Chris

Sabo and I made it a habit of taking the Number 7 train to Shea Stadium. This was back in the day before it was chic to take the Number 7. We loved it—being with all the fans and that great New York energy, aside from the fact that it was a fast and easy way to get to Shea.

Lou Piniella then instituted his famous "dress code" that required all of us to wear slacks and a dress shirt. So much for mixing with fans. The next time Chris and I got on that train to Shea Stadium, we stuck out like sore thumbs. After that we still took the train rides, but they didn't feel the same.

The camaraderie I had with third baseman Chris Sabo during my tenure with the Reds was wonderful. My roommate in spring training, he and I shared a similar tenacity. He was a fierce competitor, intense behind his goggle glasses, and he took the game as seriously as I did. We were out of the same mold, both homegrown Ohio boys who loved playing for our Reds. All Chris wanted to do was keep getting hits and helping us win ball games. My type of player.

After having a great year in 1990, Chris was a major reason we rocketed ourselves to the postseason. At twenty-seven years old, I'd had a strong year as well—hitting for an average of .270, with 16 HRs, 78 RBIs, and 14 stolen bases in 145 games.

In the National League Championship Series against the Pittsburgh Pirates—a most dramatic series—I was able to contribute with my glove by throwing out Sid Bream at second base and Andy Van Slyke at third. Those bang-bang plays that I'd dreamed about as a child had magically come to pass.

I felt like a kid again, only *this* dream was a reality.

The play at third, in the second game of that series, was the one I'll always cherish, because an outfielder takes great pride in his ability to throw out a runner at any base, but particularly at third. There is almost a feeling of a one-on-one contest. Andy was testing my arm, and I won out. When a play like that happens, there is certainly an adrenaline rush that words can't even capture. It was that play, nationally televised, that made me known to casual fans. It was typical 1990 Reds, denying runs as opposed to scoring them.

The fact that it happened at Riverfront Stadium in front of the home crowd and my entire family was an added rush.

It was a good throw, but the media made a celebrity out of me for it. Fifteen minutes of fame. All that attention for doing my job? How *embarrassing*. The next day the satellite trucks pulled up to my house, and then sports broadcaster Tim McCarver came to the door. Tim McCarver! He asked whether he could interview me.

"Sure!" I gulped. Having Tim inside my house was wild. He came on in, along with his crew, and we sat down for a filmed interview. *Man,* I thought, *I must be doing something right to have Tim McCarver sitting in my house.* Maybe luck didn't have that much to do with it.

In the fourth game of the series against Pittsburgh, with the Reds leading the series 2–1, Chris Sabo and I both homered to help Cincinnati win the game 5–3.

After winning the NLCS, the Cincinnati Reds were on their way to the World Series—an incredible team effort that I could hardly believe was really happening. Oakland was the winner of the ALCS, having made it once again to the World Series by beating Boston 4–1, winning the final four games. The A's-Sox series might have gone further had it not been for Boston's heartbreak in Game Four, when Roger Clemens was thrown out of the game at the beginning for saying something to the home-plate umpire. It was a tough loss for Boston and their fans, and I felt for them.

Oakland had the psychological boost coming into the 1990 World Series of having won it the year before, beating a tremendous Giants team in the famous Bay Area World Series, which was almost canceled by the horrific earthquake that had actually struck during a game. The quake devastated the entire Bay Area, causing the loss of lives and leaving many without homes and jobs. As with all national disasters, the country felt the economic and emotional toll, grieving along with San Francisco. But it was decided that the 1989 Series would go on, and Oakland had prevailed.

Besides the feeling from the A's that they had momentum on their side, they were a truly tough team—with formidable pitching by everyone from Bob Welch to Dennis Eckersley, the Cy Young Award winner, who had by now become legendary as a closer.

But we Reds had our own indomitable pitching going into the World Series, with "Mr. Perfect," Tom Browning, among others, as well as the famous "Nasty Boys" bullpen, the nickname given to the likes of Randy Myers, Rob Dibble, and Norm Charlton.

The A's had the double-edged sword of having their focus on winning two in a row and going for a dynasty. As I would know all too well in later years, history can often be an intangible that can make you want something so badly and drive you nuts if you fall short of accomplishing that goal.

Though I was absolutely confident we could win the Series, not in my wildest dreams did I think we had the potential to sweep the A's. And yet, after we'd won the first three games, going into Game Four, it was now a possibility.

At a critical point in the game, Lou Piniella was pacing the dugout, nervous and intent on victory.

As though a lightbulb suddenly went off, Piniella strode over to Chris Sabo to query him. "Can O'Neill bunt?" he asked, but before Chris could respond, Piniella quickly answered his own question, saying, "I guess we'll see if he can."

Up at bat, I followed that exchange by laying down a perfect bunt that was misplayed by the A's—enabling us to score a run. Once again the techniques Dad had taught me in my backyard and in Little League had come to the rescue in a critical World Series game. The bunt is a tactic that faces extinction, especially in the American League, but it can really come in handy, and it did.

Lou was most proud.

So, too, was Chick O'Neill—there for every thrilling moment, hot dog in hand—as were my brothers, who flew in to Oakland to experience my first World Series with me.

Before the games, I got Dad credentialed so he could walk around the park. He looked as though he really should have been pitching on the mound in Oakland, walking around casually like he was just one of the guys.

My brothers were also on the field for batting practice during the World Series, excited to get out there and shag fly balls with the rest of the Reds. A few things had changed since childhood, when I looked up to my brothers as baseball idols—the benchmarks for success. That came as something of a shock when it was time for them to take the field and, as though no time had passed, I expected them to play in that same ferocious style they had when I was a kid.

All of a sudden one ball ricocheted off the wall and hit my brother Mike in the face while he was attempting to field it!

"Don't quit your day jobs!" one of my coaches yelled to him in good humor.

The other change was that my brothers were no longer accusing me of cheating or of being just lucky. They recognized that more important than luck was the send-off in life I'd gotten from them and from Dad.

Back in Cincinnati, the victory parade in honor of the World Championship Reds—sweeping the A's in four games straight—marked a major pinnacle in my life as I stood on a float with thousands of people lined up to cheer us on. I was once like so many of the kids I saw that day out in the crowd. I was still that same kid, only now instead of being a face in the crowd, I had the great fortune to be one of the young players up on the float waving and thanking the hometown fans.

To say that it felt great to be in spring training in 1991 as a World Champion would be an understatement.

Throughout the season my normal intensity only seemed to increase as I pressed to do my best for the team and to keep putting up major-league numbers—a goal met with 28 home runs and 91 RBIs, though I batted .256, under what it had been the year before.

Toward the end of the summer, my tendency for being hard on myself was made blatantly clear. During a home game one night, I had been on a tear. With each of my first four times up, I got a hit. Going 4 for 4 early in the game—including one hit that was a home run—I knew I'd have another at-bat waiting for me late in the game.

In the dugout I mentally psyched myself, ready to go out to the on-deck circle, thinking about how great it would be to go 5 for 5.

The time for me to have my fifth, and final, at-bat arrived at last. With immense confidence I stood in the batter's box, crouched into my stance, and waited for my pitch. My pitch never came. Instead I took a called third strike that was about six inches off the plate—which I thought was clearly a ball. Totally upset, I trudged back to the dugout and was unable to shake that last at-bat, my blue funk hovering over me all the way home.

The phone rang, and I dejectedly answered it. Not knowing my state of mind, Joe Bick—my longtime friend and agent—had called to congratulate me. He was elated.

"Congratulations on your great night!" Joe said.

"Did you see that last pitch?" I replied in a still-flustered voice.

"Paul, you just went four for five with a home run," he said, continuing to plead his case that I had played a masterful game that night.

The conversation really brought home the way in which I could sometimes be my own worst enemy, especially right before we hung up and he asked me something that continued to puzzle me for the next eleven years.

"Why is it that all you can think about is that one bad at-bat?" Joe asked.

"I don't know," I said. I had no answer for him or for myself.

The only thing I could do, drawing from what Dad had so often encouraged me to do, was try to put my focus on the at-bats to come.

Bottom line, I refused to fault myself for really wanting to play well and for wanting to let my team know that I was trying my hardest— even when doing so came at my own expense.

Through the 1992 season, my life with the Reds felt to me like a continuing storybook fantasy come true. I was playing at home, living at home, eating dinners with my family, talking to neighbors, and heading off to Riverfront to play professional baseball. Life couldn't possibly get any better.

But, unbeknownst to me, it could get worse. Shockingly so, which in fact it did on a November day in 1992, when my baseball life as I knew it was shattered.

In retrospect there were clues that should have prepared me. Yes, there had been vague rumors going around the clubhouse about my possibly being traded, although as a player I never listened to the rumors.

The other warning signs had come from higher-ups in the Reds organization who had been insisting throughout the 1992 season that I needed to improve as a power hitter. "We want you to hit more home runs," I was told on several occasions.

That had been hard for me when my strength, reinforced by my dad, was always as a line-drive hitter. Even though I had homered plenty in my career, my calling was never as a big home-run hitter, and, when I tried to be one, I fell flat on my face. In fact, after I'd hit 28 home runs in 1991, the pressure put on me backfired, and I cut my home-run total in half in 1992. The brass didn't realize that my hitting home runs and having a terrible batting average was not in the team's best interest. My father knew better in believing and teaching me that teams win games through solid, fundamental baseball that involved hitting for average, stealing bases, and scoring runs on the little plays. Hitting home runs is wonderful if a player is that type of hitter. I wasn't. I knew my limitations—I was a hitter with power, not a power hitter.

Yet never in my worst nightmares did I think that would bring my tenure with my beloved Reds to an end.

In fact, on the November day that I revved up the lawn mower to cut the grass in the front yard, I was mentally starting to gear up for the 1993 season. Halfway through the job, I saw my wife come running out of the door, waving at me to come inside. She had to tell me something.

I ambled inside, not quite aware of any sense of urgency, and saw that Nevalee was crying. Without an explanation she played back the message that had been left on our answering machine, and there it was on tape, cold and blunt.

Jim Bowden, the Reds' general manager, had left me a message informing me that I had been traded to the New York Yankees!

Traded?

How could they be doing this to me, one of their own? And how could they be doing it in such an impersonal, insensitive manner? Replaying the message out of sheer disbelief, I listened again to Jim's voice on my machine telling me my fate in a recording, and my blissful autumn day suddenly turned into a surreal drama.

How was I supposed to react, without any preparation? Nevalee and I sat and cried for hours. Though I knew logically that these decisions came about because of several colluding factors, in my emotional heart of hearts it was a humiliation. The Reds were basically telling me to get lost, that they didn't need me anymore and had no use for me in their organization. They had messed with my mind enough in the past regarding what caliber of player I was that they had made me momentarily forget who I was and what I had accomplished. *Obviously,* I thought, *if I were any good, why would the team want to get rid of me?*

I should have guessed that Dad would have something reassuring to say about this drastic turn of events, but I couldn't have imagined the kind of reaction I got after telling him the news.

For the ultimate optimist, my announcement that I was no longer a Cincinnati Red but was being traded to the New York Yankees was regarded as one big party. The rest of us were all in tears, and my father was celebrating. "Paul," he exclaimed, "this is going to be the best thing that ever happened to you."

Yeah, right, Dad, I thought, *fathers are supposed to say that to their sons.*

But as he continued, I could hear that he wasn't just placating me. He genuinely had total confidence in what he was saying. By the end of the night, after talking to him, I actually began to get pumped up and sort of saw things his way.

After all, my father hadn't been wrong about anything that had happened to me in my entire baseball life so far. Maybe this wasn't the end of the world. Maybe he was right.

Either way I had to move forward.

Bags packed, nerves in tow, I boarded a plane that left Cincinnati and flew off into the uncertain sky. The plane was carrying me to New York City, where I was headed to meet my new boss, George Steinbrenner, bringing along my hopes that my father's words were correct.

PART

III

1992 – 2001

SEVEN

The House That Ruth Built

Dad was right. I felt it. I felt the turn of events.

Once I'd set foot inside Yankee Stadium and met with Mr. Steinbrenner and Gene Michael, I could see that a whole new baseball life was out there.

At the New York Yankees' press conference, what were once my tears of sadness over being traded now turned to tears of joy. Gene "Stick" Michael gets the thanks for pulling off the trade that sent Yankees' outfielder Roberto Kelly to the Reds and brought me and minor-league first baseman Joe DeBerry to New York. It was Gene's idea, his belief that I could help the team, that put me in a Yankee uniform.

In spite of the bleakness of the November cold in the Bronx, standing in the Stadium, I could envision the colorful and illustrious history of the ballpark I had heard about since I'd learned to read and write. This was the "House That Babe Ruth Built." The stands were empty, and the lush green grass that sparkles in the summer sun looked that day as if it were trying to hide itself in the winter, but for a midwestern boy raised on Baseball, this had the feel of the promised land.

To be able to say to family and friends that I would now be playing in the same park that Babe Ruth once called home was incredible, and quite humbling.

In announcing me at the press conference with such importance, the Yankees awed me more by stressing how much they valued me. They certainly seemed to have confidence that I could make a meaningful contribution. In the middle of the dreary day, as I looked out on to the field from the press box, with nobody in the stands and all the signs down, I could feel my nerves returning. It was the vastness of the park that got to me.

"This place is too big for me," I confided to Dad on the phone.

He laughed. "You'll do just fine there."

Nervous though I was, my spirits were definitely lifting, and more reasons to celebrate came a month later when Nevalee gave birth to our second child, Aaron, on December 21. Having another son was a dream. Now I had two-thirds of an outfield!

Another off-season flew by, full of new blessings brought by our new baby, and before I knew it, spring-training time had arrived. We headed south for Fort Lauderdale to begin our new life with a new team, training in a new Florida city.

While my enthusiasm had been steadily rising, I still couldn't get past my nervousness. I couldn't help it. After twelve seasons as a part of the Reds organization, I had developed a strong following of fans. Would the New York fans accept me? Would I prove myself, a new-comer, worthy? Dad's reassurances played in my mind like a mantra:

Everything would work out fine, and the park wasn't going to eat me alive, and the fans would take a liking to me as long as I went out and played hard each day.

That was my intention as I arrived at spring training in 1993 for a most memorable first day. Early on that day, I had the honor of being introduced to a real legendary Yankee, Don Mattingly.

Don was to be a tremendously important influence on me. Don Mattingly played the game the way it should be played. He didn't care about his endorsements or his name on billboards. He cared only about the effort he gave to the team.

There are certain people you can meet for the first time and have the strangest feeling that you've known them forever. You feel right at home, as if your values, sensibilities, even your senses of humor are cut from the same cloth. That was how it was for me when I shook Don Mattingly's hand. It felt like we were old friends getting reacquainted.

From that day to this, I can say that I have more respect for Don Mattingly than for anyone else I have ever played alongside in my entire career.

Donnie raised everyone's game and made us all look better. Here was a true athlete, a three-sport star in high school, who had won a batting title in 1984, hitting .343 that year, and who had been the MVP in 1985, not to mention the fact that he'd hit home runs in eight consecutive games in 1987.

What was his secret? His philosophy was basic—just to focus on thinking about how he could help the team to win, every night.

Before games, as other players went through every kind of conceivable preparation and ritual to get mentally and physically ready to play, Don's strategy, which he articulated many times to me was simply this: "I'm just going to go out there and be myself today."

Simple as it sounds, it worked, and it was so true of him. He never tried to be anything less than genuine, and he never tried to make himself another type of hitter besides the type he was.

With input like that from Don Mattingly, from other teammates, and from the Yankee management, any nervousness that I'd brought with me to spring training was soon gone. I was good to go, ready to go out and just be myself.

Opening Day, 1993. I had three hits in my first game in the Bronx.

Yankee Stadium was in full bloom—lush green grass, the ballpark hung with red and blue bunting. There was no better place on baseball's good earth to be.

It felt as if the fans were on top of me. Looking over my shoulder into the outfield stands, I saw the intensity of their baseball passion and heard them screaming. Cincinnati, where the fans were farther away, was a library compared to Yankee Stadium. The Astroturf back at Riverfront Stadium was a poor impostor compared to the real grass of the Bronx, and all the memories it held.

The Yankee locker room also didn't have the cliques that some teams have in their clubhouses, which I'd experienced to a certain extent with my former team. The Yankees were one big group of twenty-five guys all playing as one. At our heart was "Donnie Baseball." Many of the guys on the 1993 roster who remained on the team throughout our great run learned to play the game the right way from him.

Before coming to New York, everyone—except for my father—had talked about the pressure of playing in pinstripes, warning me about everything from the scrutiny of management to the judgment of the fans.

Amazingly, I found myself more relaxed being the new kid on a tougher block. To my relief, I was no longer playing in front of people who'd actually known me since I was a kid, who maybe had preconceived ideas about how well I could or couldn't do, who had certain expectations. In Cincinnati the feeling that I had to do something extra for all of the friends and family in the stands—hitting that home run for the buddy who came down to watch from Columbus—usually made me push too hard. Instead of hitting the homer or getting that big smash for a pal of mine, more often than not I'd strike out and look stupid doing it.

I'm probably one of the few players who found playing in New York to offer *less* pressure. A lesson learned for me. Sometimes the best thing a player can do is sign with his hometown team. And sometimes the worst thing a player can do is sign with his hometown team. It all depends on the player and the particular situation.

For me, because so much of baseball is a head game, the freedom to go out and play as if I were out there alone—just playing for myself and for Mom and Dad and my wife—was liberating. Even though there might have been fifty-five thousand people at a particular Yankees game, in what most people called a giant fishbowl, when I took to the outfield or went into the batter's box, it felt as comfortable as being in my own backyard.

This was also a great help to my batting average, which climbed with each season here.

The more comfortable I was, the better I was able to play, the greater the intensity of the appreciation that Yankee fans displayed. It was a very different atmosphere from Riverfront Stadium. Riverfront crowds were wonderful, but the House That Ruth Built *rocked* every night.

Dad was correct. This was turning out to be a blessing for me.

Another welcome feature of my Yankee journey was the American League style of baseball and getting to play in the ballparks that I'd read about as a kid but had never played in before, when I was in the National League.

A lot of the ballparks I'd been playing in were cookie-cutter stadiums that looked the same from the outside, parks like Three Rivers Stadium and Veterans Stadium. The American League had some of the last remaining shrines in baseball, with plenty of ghosts running around their historic fields—places such as Tiger Stadium, Fenway Park, and old Cleveland Stadium.

Many of the National League parks had artificial turf, while in the American League—at stadiums like Fenway, Tiger Stadium, Camden Yards, and Yankee Stadium—there was a predominance of grass. From my point of view, playing on grass makes baseball much more fun for both the fans and the players.

The American League also had some of the fiercest rivalries in sports, especially the Yankees–Red Sox one. The intensity of that rivalry surprised even me, when in 1993 I took my first walk down Yawkey Way and observed fans eating hot peanuts, talking Sox baseball, loving their team, and viciously hating the Yankees—yet in a fun, creative way. With their signs and chants, they were original and clever with their hatred. I loved it.

The passion that ran through the streets of Boston was something that touched my dad as well. He loved the road trips to Fenway Park to watch me play, remarking that he thought the Sox crowds were good baseball fans as he took his favorite spot in the stands and listened to the pregame crowd talking baseball. Naturally, he always made friends and managed to slip into a conversation the fact that he was partial because his son was playing for the New York Yankees. Fittingly, Dad's last baseball road trip was to Fenway, with Robert, braving an incredibly sultry summer in 1998.

As intense as the New York fans, the Boston fans also rocked Fenway with their cheers for Roger Clemens and Mo Vaughn, rooting for their beloved Red Sox. The vendors all lined the streets, and the Fenway Faithful wore their O'NEILL SUCKS! T-shirts, which were being sold before games at the concession stands along Yawkey Way and Ted Williams Way. It was never personal, always just a Sox–Yankees thing. I, as an opposing player, could only tip my cap to them for their loyalty.

This made it all the more impressive when the Yankee fans made the trek to Boston for the away games and were bold enough to cheer like nuts for us in the bleachers! I'll give any Yankee fan the nod when that fan tells me he or she survived wearing a Yankees jersey in the right-center-field bleachers at Fenway Park.

At the team hotel, I couldn't believe how many fans came over to us from New York to say they'd made the road trip just to watch us play. They weren't there on vacation or in town for business. They were in Boston to watch us play the Sox. It was amazing and touching, something I hadn't witnessed to that extent before.

During my first visits to Fenway, the Yankees had me patrolling left field, not right field, and after having heard all the hype, I found myself smack up against Fenway's famous "Green Monster." The nickname is 100 percent apropos, because the wall *is* a monster. The caroms off it are as strange as any I've ever seen. That wall truly has a mind of its own.

Early in the day, I used batting practice as an opportunity to try to learn to read that wall. With hit after hit off it, I practiced trying to catch the ball, and each time the ball caromed off in a different direction. The hype was justified as far as I was concerned. The Green Monster really is a phenomenon. Of course, there were two facets to this wall: how the wall played and what lay behind the wall. Curiosity already had me as to the former, but it even caught up with me as to the latter.

Like many a ballplayer before me who dared to investigate, I knew that I had to venture behind the Green Monster to satisfy my curiosity as to what lay beyond, and so one day during batting practice, I stepped through the open door—and all my questions were suddenly answered.

The Green Monster's hallowed corridor is best described as follows: Imagine you've entered your grandmother's old basement, and you've just inhaled a whiff of the cool, damp cellar air. The Monster has that dank smell to it that's overpowering. Not so much dusty, but rather a moldy smell of moisture and mold from the runoff of water over the old dirt that had collected underneath it over the years. This is a familiar ballpark smell that varies in degree but is recognizable to all ballplayers. They'll go to a particular public place, and the smell will remind them of some ballpark.

Fenway Park is a wacky ballpark in general. I love the park, but weird things happen there when it comes to the actual ball game, things that just don't occur in other parks. Maybe it's the Fenway mystique or the Green Monster phenomenon. Or both.

Whatever it is, after several bizarre experiences, I came to the conclusion that literally no lead is safe at Fenway. We'd been down going into the late innings by so many runs that everyone in the world thought the game was over. The lead was so tilted in favor of the Red Sox that you could almost hear what the Boston fans were thinking: *Just get it over with.*

Suddenly, in the twinkling of an eye, with a wily carom off the wall here and a kooky bounce there, we had brought ourselves back in the game with a chance to actually win it.

That had been the scenario for the memorable Bucky Dent home run in 1978 that gave the Yankees the win in that historic one-game playoff. It was inexplicable.

More than once or twice at Fenway Park after the game—win or lose—I found myself coming into the locker room, throwing my spikes into my locker, watching the dirt fly off, and asking myself, *What in the world happened out there today?*

Detroit's Tiger Stadium was another treat for all its nostalgia. When I entered the park for the first time, I immediately remembered watching the Reggie Jackson home run in the All-Star Game on TV with my brothers. Ernie Harwell, the legendary broadcaster, was also there—a huge part of Tigers history.

One of the most interesting features of playing in Tiger Stadium was the close proximity of the fans to right field. I could have done without the barrage of "you suck" and their telling me how bad we were even though we were winning, but it was fun to be able to actually hear comments and place the voice to the face when I looked over.

The dugouts had ceilings that were six feet in height, at least on the visiting side, and for a six-foot-four-inch guy like me, that meant hitting my head every time I forgot to duck as I ran out onto the field to take my position.

Aside from those quirks, the history and the ambience of Tiger Stadium made it a treasure to me. The porches in right field and left field were like no other ballpark. Standing in the real grass of the outfield, I felt the character of this neighborhood park and was proud to be here.

Life was good. Rye, the town where we lived in Westchester County, was quiet and beautiful, a quick drive to the Bronx and a great place to raise kids. The people of the community took so much pride in being family-oriented that they actually scheduled play time on a community board for parents. Given my schedule and my desire to be with my wife and kids as much as possible, Rye provided just the right setting.

During our first year, Nevalee made a lot of new friends, who have since become lifelong friends, and she also traveled with me more than the average baseball wife did.

This was the year when Jim Abbott pitched a no-hitter against the Cleveland Indians, getting Carlos Baerga to ground out to short for the final out. When I saw Randy Velarde throw the ball to first base and Don Mattingly jump up in the air, I was part of the collective gasp that shook the entire ballpark.

I really liked Jim as a player and as a person, and I'd rooted for him since his first year in the big leagues. Because he had the use of only one full arm and hand, he had to hold the glove on his nonthrowing partial arm, deliver the throw to home plate, and then switch the glove back to his hand to be able to catch a possible comebacker to the mound. The velocity of those mechanics was superhuman. The way he made history that day was unbelievable.

To go through what Jim went through in his career with his disability and to be as positive about life and about baseball as he was showed me what he was all about. He had the heart of a true champion.

I ran into the infield to join the party. Incredible. Jim Abbott had just thrown a no-hitter in Yankee Stadium!

After more exhilarating moments like that one, I finished a great first season with a .311 batting average, excited about the upcoming 1994 season.

The sense that we were going places was apparent as the year got under way. Looking back in later years, I can say that it was 1994 that turned the page for the Yankees ball club as a franchise. The team embodied the essence of camaraderie for me, with guys like Don Mattingly, Mike Gallego, Mike Stanley, Randy Velarde, and Jim Leyritz making that year really enjoyable. Jimmy Key was another fantastic teammate, as was Wade Boggs.

We battled as a team, and we won because of that cohesiveness. It's the only way to explain how we were winning games against teams who, I knew in my heart, were better than we were. But when all was said and done, the Yankees were the ones who came away with the "W" when the game was over. Playing fundamentally sound baseball, this year the team chemistry just clicked—the beginning of what the press wrote so much about in later years.

Though, unbeknownst to any of us, the season was to be a shortened one, it was definitely to be a banner year for me as a batter. Great Yankee management had helped make the difference, starting back when I'd first arrived and talked to some of the coaches about how to better prepare myself for a game. In the same way that Dad had always sought to accentuate the positive, their advice was for me to work by visualizing my upcoming at-bats, suggesting I review my good at-bats before a game to see how things had gone right the night before. The idea was, that's what I should be copying. I listened, taking the advice to heart.

After hitting well my first season, I stayed with the system. Before each game I watched footage of my previous at-bats as part of my pregame routine—fifteen minutes of videotapes showing good swing after good swing. Pretty soon I learned to replay those tapes in my mind, allowing me to visualize just how I wanted to hit the ball as I approached the plate—often taking away an opposing pitcher's game plan. With my focus trained only on my good swings, it took away the guesswork and uncertainty of being outpsyched by a pitcher or having to look for specific pitches to hit.

Visualization, practice, preparation, and focus were baseball fundamentals my father had first taught me, now taken to the next level. Perfectionist that I was, however, I was so obsessed that I developed the habit of visualizing and practicing my swing *everywhere,* even out in right field. This was to be a running joke in later years, when television cameras eventually caught up with me. Maybe, besides being a product of my compulsiveness about my swing, it might have also had something to do with having too much idle time in right field.

Admittedly, I had my other quirks—which, by the way, come with the baseball territory. One of mine had to do with my selection of the ultimate baseball bat and how my bats came to bear the consequences of my daily ritual, the center of another running line of jokes over the years.

A player's baseball bat is a very personal item, not a subject that major-leaguers take lightly. Players go to the ends of the country to find the bat that's right for them. Not only that, but for me, as my father's son and as an O'Neill brother, having the best sports equipment, personally customized, was important to my game.

When I came to the Yankees the year before, in 1993, I changed bats and started using a C243. A real heavy bat—thirty-five inches, thirty-five ounces—it was a Louisville Slugger made of ash wood. A lot would be written in the coming years—when the home-run races brought much greater scrutiny to the variations in bats—about which player used what kind of wood. Some were quoted as swearing by ash, while others said they wouldn't touch anything other than maple.

I had tried some maple bats, and I found out later that Mo Vaughn and other great hitters use these bats, and they were okay. But I was so comfortable with my ash bat that I could never walk away from it. I liked the way it felt in my hands and the way the label looked. There was also the very specific design I used in taping my bat—which many fans noticed with amusement—a crazy pattern that I'd learned from Dave Concepcion when we were both in Cincinnati. When I tried taping the bat as he did, I got used to it, from both a physical and a psychological standpoint. The grip had a specific feel that empowered me, for whatever reason, and to change it would have unnerved me.

Any baseball player knows that a good bat becomes, as they say, like a pair of well-worn jeans. The bat, once used for a couple of weeks, becomes so comfortable in your hands and throughout your swing that it's connected to how you hit. A combination of feel and aesthetics. The pine tar starts to get that really tarry look, as if it has been worn for ages, and it gets stickier, and the grip feels better and better with every swing.

My teammate Danny Tartabull, a powerful, outstanding hitter, came over to me one day and picked up my bat, gripped it tightly, took a few practice swings, and said, "Paul, that's a Bam-Bam club!"

We cracked up over the image of Bam-Bam in the *Flintstones* cartoons banging his oversize prehistoric bat down on the floor to get everyone's attention, his little-kid voice knowing how to say only, "Bam-Bam! Bam-Bam!"

Danny was a big guy, so he could swing the club without a problem, but even he used a lighter bat than I did.

Bam-Bam club or not, I stuck by my Louisville Slugger throughout my career in New York. A lot of players are superstitious, believing that once they become comfortable with a bat, it's bad luck to change it. My feeling was, why fix it, if it ain't broke?

Danny joked about my being Bam-Bam and about my pregame routine that included sitting in my chair for an hour holding my bat in my hands and taking little half swings.

"What are you going to do when you quit playing and you don't have that chair anymore?" he'd ask me and laugh. Danny was one of the guys I loved being around, because he loosened me up, and that was something an intense guy like me needed.

I also picked up the habit—not uncommon for ballplayers—of

banging the bat on my cleats, although I may have carried it to an extreme. But there was a method to my madness. The more I banged a bat against my cleats, knocking out the dirt and grass, the more I chipped out big chunks of wood from the bat. That way I could look at a bat and judge by the bites taken out of it by my cleats how long I'd been using it.

Despite the kidding I got for my various idiosyncrasies, nobody really gave me a hard time. Whatever works. And it worked for the 1994 season, when I was batting over and around .400 for the first three months and coming away with an average of .359 for the abridged season, earning the American League batting title for the year. It was significant as an achievement for hard work, but what pleased me most was the feeling that it validated the Yankees' faith in me, along with seeing the pride that Dad took in my winning the title.

In the meantime my team had been cooking as the regular season approached its end. We were atop the American League East, and by early August were distancing ourselves from everyone else. The National League had its own feel-good story that centered on the Montreal Expos, who were in first place, with Felipe Alou at the helm.

This happy state would turn sour when labor talks threatened to cancel the rest of the season. By the All-Star Game in Pittsburgh, it was apparent that both sides were not about to reach a compromise and that there was a possibility that games would be canceled. What a tough pill to swallow for me. The Yankees were having a dream year—tops in our division and the best record in the American League—and I was batting better than I had ever batted in my career.

Although we weren't yet the stellar team that we became in 1996, in the 1994 season we were winning ball games the way World Series champions are supposed to win them—thanks to manager Buck Showalter, who'd done a fantastic job heading us in the right direction.

Don Mattingly got major credit, too, as a great on-field presence and an unrivaled leader in the clubhouse.

Ironically, I had just left Cincinnati, where, even though we'd won the World Series in 1990, we were beginning to fall apart as a franchise, my departure coming just before the start of a further downslide. In a stroke of good timing, I'd come to New York at the right juncture, one that allowed me to ride on the coattails of the Yankee momentum and even to help energize it. Now, all of a sudden, there was a work stoppage, a strike. The unthinkable was happening.

The strike of 1994 sent me home in August, a foreign experience. I'd never been home in August since the summer before my senior year of high school, fourteen years earlier. I didn't know what to do with myself. I'd wake up every morning and have to wait for phone calls and listen to the radio like everyone else to find out what was going on with the negotiations. Each day that passed brought an escalating degree of shock to my mind. Never in my wildest thoughts, even in a worst-case scenario, at least in August, did I think the World Series would be canceled. The mere idea of canceling the rest of the season seemed ridiculous.

I'd get up every day with this uneasy feeling, reminding myself that if we went back to play the next day, or in a few days, I had to be ready, both physically and mentally.

As a player, once you turn off that switch inside you, it takes an entire off-season and the start of spring training to turn everything on again. You can't turn it off for a week and then show up and expect your body to play in top form as you have for years. It won't work. I worried constantly about the impact that a prolonged strike could have on our team. The mental part of playing every day is just as important, because without use it, too, can become stale and out of kilter and have lasting ill effects on your game.

My coping skill was to wake up and train as if I were going to make that drive from Westchester to Yankee Stadium. I'd lift weights in the morning, I'd run, and I'd go out and take as many swings as I would during a regular day of batting practice.

Then came word that the balance of the season was officially canceled. What a disaster! The rest of August and all of September had been wiped out. But the real shocker was the news that soon followed, only days later. I was sitting at home, and there on the television was Bud Selig with an official announcement from Major League Baseball.

When Selig announced in those next moments that Major League Baseball had canceled the World Series, I was both shocked and disappointed. It was a blunder, and one of the darkest moments in baseball.

Never before had the World Series been canceled. Two world wars, natural disasters, economic crises, and worse had never been occasions to cancel a World Series, and now in 1994, astonishingly, labor problems had brought the game to its knees.

For me one of the very few silver linings to this dark cloud was that in desperation for something to do with myself, I rekindled my love for playing drums, and since then I've continued to play regularly. After some lessons from Doug Mayo, a good friend and Cincinnati music-store owner, I mastered a killer rendition of the Stones' "Honky Tonk Woman." Being the competitive guy I am, after that song became the first that I could drum straight through from memory, I started thinking like I'd gotten a hit record in the music business. I was ready to go on tour and kick Charlie Watts off his throne!

While that was in the realm of fantasy, I actually had an opportunity to make my television acting debut on the most popular sitcom of the 1990s when I received a call from Jerry Seinfeld. He'd called to invite me to appear on *Seinfeld* in a guest spot, proposing that the studio arrange to fly me and Nevalee out to Burbank, California, where they'd

shoot the episode. Up until the strike, I'd never had much time to follow TV and had no idea what a hot show this was. Moreover, it concerned me how the fans would react to a ballplayer's appearing on
television during the strike.

Declining politely, I told him, "No thanks," and thought no more of
it until I mentioned it offhandedly to Mom and Dad.

They were stunned. You did what? They couldn't believe I'd turned
down *Seinfeld*! In news to me, it so happened that my mother and
father were huge fans of the show, watched it all the time, and thought
I was nuts for turning Jerry down. You'll never be offered the opportunity again, my folks told me, saying in essence, *Paul, you blew it!*

After that, just out of curiosity, I decided to check out what the fuss
was all about and why everybody loved the show so much. The neurotic
humor and the offbeat New York characters won me over immediately,
and pretty soon, I was hooked on *Seinfeld*. That's when it hit me why
my parents were so up in arms. They were right—it was a big missed
opportunity. Jerry, of course, wouldn't ask me again. I had really blown
it! Or so I thought. Yogi Berra's famous words applied here too: "It ain't
over till it's over."

The strike concerned me deeply on another front: What would happen to the players in terms of the fans? The special relationship
between ballplayers and fans was something my father taught me to
honor. I wanted to be loved by the fans. I wanted their cheers. Their
applause mattered to me. In return I wanted to be a gracious athlete
and to carry myself as someone worthy of their applause.

My image had been important to me long before I came to New
York, but I knew even before 1994, when I played my first ball game
alongside Don Mattingly, that something important was happening for
me here with the Yankees, and I didn't want to ruin it.

Then came my contract negotiations. When I was traded to the

Yankees from the Reds in November of 1992, I was in the middle of a three-year contract. The Yankee organization picked up the final years on the contract, which were at their end here at the close of the 1994 season, coinciding, as it happened, with the strike. The Yankees wanted to lock me in to a long-term deal, which was exactly what I wanted. My great wish was to play every game for the rest of my career with the New York Yankees.

When Joe Bick, my agent and valued friend, called to tell me what the Yankees had in mind in negotiating my new contract, I was completely taken aback.

"So, Paul," Joe began, "what would you say you're worth?"

"What do you think I'm worth?" I asked him in response.

"Between 5.25 and 5.5 million dollars a year, about a 21, 22 million-dollar package over four years." Joe said it so matter-of-factly, I waited to see if he was kidding.

When I saw that he wasn't, I said, "Oh, God, that's embarrassing. That's just plain too much money. That puts me in the 'greed' category. If it's four years, keep it under 20 million."

My father always laughed about the sports salaries that had been steadily rising to astronomical levels over the years, partly because he came from an era when athletes had traditionally been underpaid. As much as he revered baseball, it was hard for him to believe that anyone could make that much money for playing a kid's game. Dad asked, "Did you ever think you'd make this type of money just playing ball?"

Not really, I told him.

Even so, Dad was of the opinion that playing for the Yankees was a blessing and that if they offered me a good deal, I should take it.

Joe completed the negotiations, and I was all set for 1995, assuming there'd be baseball. The contract was for four years, a total of $19.9 million.

Dad, twenty-nine-years old, just back from military service, looking young, strong, and handsome in 1949. *(O'Neill family photograph)*

Chick and the O'Neill brothers in Dad's home state of Nebraska during a family reunion in 1966. *(Left to right)* Paul and Kevin in front, with Pat, Robert, and Mike behind them. *(O'Neill family photograph)*

Dressed up on our family vacation on Singer Island, Florida, in 1967. Yours truly front and center, in an outfit I'd rather forget, with *(left to right)* Mike, Pat, Robert, Kevin, and Dad, Mom, and Molly in the back wondering what's going to happen next! *(O'Neill family photograph)*

Hanging on the rail in the upper deck of old Crosley Field in Cincinnati with one of my idols, Roberto Clemente, out in right field. Clemente's number 21 became significant years later when the Reds assigned that number to me. This photo was taken during the 1968 season. *(O'Neill family photograph)*

The infamous Julian Speer A's, champs of the Plain City Tournament in 1973. I was ten and this was a special experience for me because I got to play on the same team with my brother Robert *(front row, far right)*, who was twelve, and Dad *(back row, far left)*, who was our coach. *(O'Neill family photograph)*

This was our homecoming dance at Brookhaven High School in Columbus, Ohio, in 1980. I was sporting my brother Kevin's hand-me-down corduroy suit! *(O'Neill family photograph)*

My first full season in AA in Burlington, Vermont, in 1984. The Reds had added me to their 40-man Major League roster prior to this season, so I felt like I was making the kind of progress I had hoped for in my career. *(O'Neill family photograph)*

Nevalee and I leaving Maize Road Methodist Church in Columbus following our wedding ceremony on December 29, 1984. My brother Mike was my best man; Nevalee's sister, Cheryl Warner, was matron of honor; and friend Cindy Noble, maid of honor. After four minor league seasons apart, we were finally together forever! *(O'Neill family photograph)*

Dad and I outside the stadium in Mayaguez, Puerto Rico, during the 1985 winter ball season. He always loved those road trips! *(O'Neill family photograph)*

Sneaking a peek over the top of the dugout during winter ball in Mayaguez, Puerto Rico, in 1985. While winter ball can be a grind following a full regular season, it can also be an important step for a young player trying to establish himself in the Major Leagues. (*O'Neill family photograph*)

Sister Molly and I grab a seat in the Yankee Stadium dugout after the press conference announcing my being traded to the Yankees on November 3, 1992. Molly, at the time of the trade, was the food critic for the *New York Times*. (*O'Neill family photograph*)

Me in 1987, during the early days in Cincinnati and the first year I spent most of the season as a Major Leaguer. It was such a thrill to finally feel like I was part of the team I grew up rooting for. (*O'Neill family photograph*)

Reds photo: Lou Piniella, Barry Larkin, and Billy Hatcher greet me as lineups are introduced for the 1990 World Series, my first trip to the postseason classic. What an experience! After leading our division "wire-to-wire" the entire season, we then beat Pittsburgh in an exciting National League Championship Series and swept Oakland for the World Championship. (*courtesy of the Cincinnati Reds*)

One of the many occasions Bernie Williams and I got to celebrate exciting Yankee moments. Playing with Bernie was a pleasure both on and off the field. His tremendous playing abilities, and the fact that he is also an accomplished musician and a fine person, made him an ideal teammate. *(Tomasso DeRosa/TDSI)*

Derek Jeter, joining the team on a full-time basis in 1996, added another significant weapon to the Yankee arsenal and solidified our lineup for the amazing success we had from 1996 through 2001. His sensational ability and work ethic had much to do with our becoming a great team. *(Tomasso DeRosa/TDSI)*

There's nothing like celebrating a World Championship in New York, and I was fortunate enough to repeat this scene four times! The feeling of riding through the "Canyon of Heroes" before hundreds of thousands of screaming Yankee fans and then hoisting the World Series Trophy in the shadows of City Hall is absolutely the greatest thrill any athlete could ever hope for. *(Tomasso DeRosa/TDSI)*

At home in Cincinnati with my father, relishing my first World Championship with the Yankees in 1996. (*O'Neill family photograph*)

A pre-workout stretch in spring training is a good time to get loose and enjoy teammates' stories about their activities the previous winter. Chuck Knoblauch and I get ready for another day while spring instructor, Mickey Rivers, checks out the troops. *(Diamond Images®)*

A dugout chat with Don Zimmer is the highlight of any day. While most of these occasions with Zim were a time to laugh at his endless, hilarious stories, I always listened closely when we discussed serious baseball. I have the greatest respect for what he knows about the game. (*Diamond Images®*)

Greeting Darryl Strawberry at home plate following a grand slam during the amazing 1998 season. Straw had a knack for big hits throughout his career, and this year was certainly no exception. While Straw's time with the Yankees was relatively short, our fans loved and supported him through good times and bad. *(Diamond Images®)*

An all-too-familiar scene of me disagreeing with an umpire!
Umpires have an extremely difficult job, but in the vast majority
of the cases, they do it very well. Strangely enough, I never won
any such disagreement! *(Diamond Images®)*

The fans of New York were always wonderful to me, and I always enjoyed when time allowed for an impromptu autograph session. Signing for fans, especially young kids, gave me a great deal of pleasure. (*Diamond Images*®)

To my horror, at the start of the 1995 season, *USA Today* published the salaries of all the players, and in prominent, bold letters up toward the top, there was my name. Contrary to what some may think, ballplayers *do* read the papers. Though I'm sure other players were going through the same upset I was, it didn't make me feel any less mortified.

My salary was published at $5.2 million for the '95 season. I flipped. Apparently, the Major League Baseball Players Association reported a portion of my signing bonus as part of the year's salary, pushing the '95 salary above the $5 million mark. Meanwhile I'd been going nuts already over receiving what I thought was too much money.

Dad had long ago instilled values in me that had shaped my philosophy of not wanting to show the fans up. What mattered most was to take what life gave you and to be thankful, not to show off, not to showboat, not to put yourself on a pedestal. The last thing I ever wanted was for fans to think of me as a greedy athlete who cared about his contract above all. My goal was never to be the highest-paid player. I wasn't about the terms of the deal. I was all about the game, and playing for the love of it.

Some so-called marquee athletes are motivated to be touted as the best, to have the biggest endorsement deals, and to appear on the greatest number of billboards. What motivated me was not the hype and the praise—which actually tended to embarrass me. My joy was excelling on the field, letting my numbers speak for themselves. Most important, I cared about winning as a team. I took my cue from Donnie Baseball: The best way to be liked by the fans was for them to see me play hard every day, in uniform.

The Yankees, I believe, appreciated the way I felt, and from then on, renewing my contract was done quietly and smoothly through Joe Bick, without any press coverage, because that was the way we wanted it.

The Yankees were wonderful to me, and I greatly appreciated Mr. Steinbrenner's generosity toward me.

In early February 1995, I went down to Fort Lauderdale—for what would be the Yankees' last year there—in order to be on hand so that when the labor dispute was resolved, I'd be ready for spring training, which we expected to begin, as usual, by March. In what was yet another strange twist in the road, players weren't allowed to go to the ballpark, even as the talks dragged on through February and into March.

Other than that I was worried about when we'd get to play again, I was bothered by my chronic habit of putting pressure on myself. After all, I would be starting a new and extremely lucrative contract, and I had no idea how the fans might feel toward me and the rest of the players once the season began. Questions ran rampant in my mind: Would there be only two thousand fans in the seats? Would there be team allegiance anymore? Would the game survive?

A break in the clouds came for me in the form of an unforgettable Billy Joel–Elton John concert in March that Nevalee and I went to see, along with Pat Kelly and his then girlfriend (who has since become his wife). Song after song sent chills down my spine and brought us to our feet, joining with the roaring crowd for those two legendary Piano Men. For those hours I completely forgot my baseball blues and just how badly I was itching to play once more.

Finally the strike was over, making April the start of spring training, and as soon as I heard the news, I was at the ballpark the very next day. At first it was a little eerie, returning from the longest break that many of us had been through in years. But that feeling passed almost instantaneously as players and coaches reunited, ready to pick up the pieces and take care of our unfinished business—making the playoffs and being that team of destiny that we knew we could be, to go all the way and win the 1995 World Series.

Our biggest weapon was Don Mattingly, a player who showed up every night and played his game: He hit for average, he hit for power, and he had the best glove in the game, maybe ever, at first base. Mattingly was the official captain of the Yankees for a reason. A captain is both an on-field and off-the-field leader, bringing the clubhouse together, settling problems that arise. Donnie did all that, but in his own way—not by getting in anyone's face, not by being demonstrative or excessively chummy in the clubhouse. He was the epitome of leading by example, and his accomplishments were the biggest stick any captain could ever carry.

The 1995 season saw outfielder and switch-hitter Bernie Williams really break onto the scene. He had great range, great instincts, and he also was inspired by Donnie—whom he admired and who appreciated his admiration—raising Bernie's own standards with his terrific swing that season to become a perennial .300 hitter. This season was an important building block for Bernie in many respects, and Donnie helped Bernie in his transformation from an everyday player at the major-league level to a full-fledged superstar.

Donnie's influence on all of us who continued with the Yankees after he retired was major. We learned just by watching Donnie play the game.

As the song says about New York, "If you can make it there, you'll make it anywhere." And for a ballplayer, if you're successful in New York, there's no better place to be in the baseball world. At least that's how I was feeling as 1995 blessedly got under way. The fans were back in the stands, and it seemed all my worries had been for naught.

But then, for reasons that were beyond me, while the Yankees were in great shape, I was beset by a slump that plagued me throughout the latter part of August. Buck Showalter knew I'd break out of it. Every-one knew it, except me.

All the ghosts of slumps past taunted me, putting the notion in my head that because I was in the middle of a bad hitting streak, it would never end. Buck watched me as, out of desperation, I even tried to bunt my way to first base once—at a moment when bunting was nei-ther called for nor successful. Head down and furious with myself, I trudged back to the dugout as Buck just shook his head at my futile bunt attempt.

He wasn't concerned, he told me. Completely confident, he said he knew things would turn around for me.

But when? The anxiety of wondering with every at-bat if this would finally be the at-bat that would be a hit—and end the protracted slump—was excruciating.

What I needed was a big game, and on August 31, 1995, in a series against the California Angels (as they were then called), opportunity knocked.

That night in Yankee Stadium, early in the game, for my first at-bat with two runners on base—imagining myself in that comfort zone of playing in my own backyard, aiming to hit right on the button—I saw the ball, hit it, and could tell from the sound that it was gone. A three-run home run! The roar that went up from the fans was thunderous. The way they continued cheering long after the dust had literally set-tled was the most incredible display of affection in the world, I thought at the time.

The sheer relief of breaking out of my slump was just what the doc-tor ordered. Needless to say, I was a little more relaxed my next time up at bat—again with two runners on base—and again I hit another hard shot. Another three-run homer! If the fans could have been any more ecstatic, I couldn't imagine it.

This was getting scary. I wasn't a home-run hitter, and now I had just hit two three-run homers in one game. And, with at least one more at-bat coming to me, the night was still young! My third time up to the plate, no runners on base, I hit a solo shot that sailed out of there.

When the night was over, I had three home runs—the only time I accomplished such a feat in one game in my career—and 8 RBIs in our victory.

In a game earlier in the season, Mike Stanley had hit three home runs off Charles Nagy of the Indians, and I cheered my brains out for him. Now I had joined Mike in the small group of players who'd hit three home runs in one game.

What I remember most was a feeling of gratitude and a feeling of wanting to soak it in and savor it.

The phone didn't have to ring that night, but it did. From the sound of the celebratory jingling, I could tell that congratulations were on their way from Dad. Hearing his upbeat voice reminded me of the countless late-night calls when things weren't going so well, or when he'd seen me visibly upset. The nights when I failed at the plate and he called me were what mattered most, when he really was in my corner. It's easy to be a fair-weather fan, much harder to offer solace during the tougher streaks, and even harder for people to walk over to you and tell you things will turn around when no guarantees say they will. Dad did all those things for me, constantly, so it was gratifying to be able to celebrate the good times.

Second chances must have been in the wind in that 1995 season, because Jerry Seinfeld came to me again and asked me to be on the show.

This time I wasn't missing the opportunity for the world. It was very flattering, and I told the *Seinfeld* folks so. We shot the episode while I was with the Yankees in California playing the Angels. A driver came to the team hotel to pick up Nevalee and me, delivering us to the studio lot in Burbank where the sitcom was shot. My scene was with Michael Richards—a master of physical comedy—who played Kramer, Jerry's kooky neighbor.

In the script, after Kramer promises a kid in the hospital that Paul O'Neill will get a couple of home runs for him, the story follows Kramer coming into the Yankee locker room, where I, playing myself, bawl him out for being in the clubhouse. When he tells me what he has committed me to doing, my line—not exactly a stretch for me—is, "I'm not a home-run hitter. Why did you promise him that?"

The whole show ended up being hilarious. Getting to hang out with the *Seinfeld* cast—Jerry Seinfeld, Michael Richards, Jason Alexander, and Julia Louis-Dreyfus, aka Jerry, Kramer, George, and Elaine—was a blast.

After it aired, it seemed that whenever male fans approached me, they wanted to talk baseball, while their wives wanted to talk about my *Seinfeld* appearance. The power of television was pretty mighty. What a fun experience to be made to feel like some movie star when I wasn't. To have fans for something besides baseball was a trip—especially for that brief cameo.

George Steinbrenner had his own sort of appearances on *Seinfeld*, played by someone who looked like him—from the back. Throughout all the story lines that had George Costanza working for Steinbrenner, you never saw the face of the famous Yankees owner.

At the end of the 1995 season, Steinbrenner—after being out of the loop due to being under suspension by Major League Baseball—was back in the Bronx on a regular basis. George was both an owner and a fan, and he loved this team and was as thrilled as we all were for the playoffs against Seattle.

Even during batting practice, when I walked onto the field to stretch, I looked around the stadium and sensed a special feeling in the air. The fact that we were playing the Mariners made it all the more dramatic, since former Yankee Lou Piniella—having left the Reds the same year I was traded to the Yankees—was now Seattle's manager and had built that team into a year-in, year-out contender. Whenever anyone goes up against a former team, the adrenaline runs wild on both sides. I was sure Lou wanted badly to win, not just to win the playoffs but to be able to say he beat the Yankees.

Whenever we faced the Mariners, much was made in the press about my relationship with Lou. In coaching his players against us, maybe because he had managed me with the Reds, he knew how to get inside my head at times.

The Yankee fans, however, stuck up for me—me personally—when it came to our rivalry with Seattle. The idea that these games had extra meaning because Lou was the manager was never in my mind. I viewed them as important because the Mariners were always a top team, and if we wanted to call ourselves the best in baseball, we needed to keep winning and beating teams like them.

It did seem odd, though, that when the Yankees and Seattle Mariners did hook up for the big games, I was always ducking pitches! At times it may even have seemed as if there was some kind of intent on those pitches that went behind my back, over my head, under my chin, with the jet stream from the ball enough to give me wind burn.

Lou may have thought that by knocking me down in the batter's box or by hitting me with a pitch it would take me out of my game plan. Maybe it was to rattle me. Who knew if this was his strategy, or if the media blew it up a bit? I do remember getting knocked down quite a lot, and then I remember its stopping after we retaliated and hit Mariner Ken Griffey Jr. That's the way baseball is, for better or for worse.

I have seen Lou many times after that, and things were always fine between us as people. It was just about winning. He wanted to win, and I wanted to win. We were now just on different sides of the diamond.

Fortunately, in Game One of the playoffs in 1995, we were on Yankee soil.

Nevalee was in the stands that night, as she had been for all my playoff games when I was with the Reds, and she noticed the heightened electricity of a stadium that was naturally intense. The fans really let out a ground-shaking roar when Bob Sheppard's introduction came for Donnie Baseball and Donnie stepped onto the field. Yankee fans, so connected to their team, knew that Donnie was the impetus that drove us all to achieve what we did this year—and, later, to what we finished in 1996. The cheering went on and on, the crowd acknowledging their awareness of how long it had taken him to get to a playoff game, to hear his name announced in the pregame ceremony, and to be able to look at playoff bunting all around the stadium walls.

Yankee Stadium that night was louder than I'd ever heard it. Raucous. There weren't any suits or ties at the ballpark that night, not like the more corporate look of later years. These were the real Yankee fans, the ones who had suffered fourteen years of not hosting a playoff series.

With Donnie leading the way, we won Game One. He didn't miss his chance to get a big single, as well as two RBIs. He had waited for this moment. It belonged to him as much as it did to the team.

In Game Two he brought the stadium to its feet and sent everyone into a state of pandemonium when he homered in the sixth inning.

Up 2–0 for the playoffs, we flew out to Seattle in high spirits. Buck Showalter was thrilled for Donnie. Buck was another person who had given this team his all. For the years that I had been in New York, Buck arrived at the ballpark at noon every single day. He had scouting reports and statistics on all of the opposing pitchers and hitters—giving us, as a team, an arsenal of information. Buck had a strategy for every possible outcome. He was prepared for us to win the whole thing and go on to the ALCS and, hopefully, the World Series.

It just didn't happen that way.

We were ahead two games to none and then lost the series. It was a devastating loss for me, as if the series had been stolen right out from under us. I felt sorry for Donnie, but he took it in stride. Against the odds, even with back injuries, he had played in a great amount of pain.

After the last game in Seattle—with the Mariners celebrating like mad—I went to find Nevalee, who was pregnant at the time with our third child. I spotted her standing in a brown maternity outfit and walked toward her, so despondent that she knew from my face I was in shock from the loss.

The plane ride home was an especially long one. Trips home after losses usually are long, with all those hours of coast-to-coast flight time to ponder what might have been if things had turned another way in the game. Most of us must have been having the same thoughts on the return flight from Seattle. What could have been?

During the flight home, Donnie hinted to me that he had just played his last game. He was satisfied with his illustrious career, and he had experienced the playoffs and shined in them. He *knew* that he could meet the playoff challenge. He *knew* that he could do it all in baseball. Bernie and I both took solace in the fact that Donnie was at peace with his decision to retire. If we had seen him broken or beaten, then it would have bothered us, because we looked up to him so much. But from what we could see, he seemed comfortable with his decision in every way.

He never had regrets about his decision, he later told us. When he officially made his announcement and quit the game, he reiterated that he was satisfied with what he had in life and with what he had accomplished in baseball.

Buck was sad to see him go, and little did we know that Buck would be headed off to Arizona and that we'd have a new skipper. The time that Buck spent with me during my early years with the Yankees helped me a great deal as a ballplayer. After a third year in pinstripes, I finished the 1995 season with a .300 batting average, and had collected 22 HRs and 96 RBIs. What was startling was when I was informed that I had become the first Yankee to lead the club in home runs and RBIs in consecutive seasons, a record not attained since Don Mattingly, when he led in both categories in the 1985 and 1986 seasons. Just to be mentioned in connection with Don Mattingly in any accomplishment was the highest honor.

Not enough praise can be heaped on Don Mattingly, who will forever be the paradigm of consistency. He was the ultimate competitor, a superior ballplayer, and the best teammate.

Six years later I would appreciate even more the example Donnie had set for me in how graciously he took his last bow. Often I would reflect back on the way I saw him in the playoffs against Seattle, watching him from the outfield as he came to take his place at first base.

He just looks so right out here, I thought, with his uniform dirty and his eye black on, a player who deserved so much attention but never asked for it.

That's how I would always remember him.

———— • ————

EIGHT

Joe Torre's Yankees

Our home team was growing. Nevalee and I planned our pregnancies so that we'd have kids in the off-season. That way we had more time to be a family, something I felt was important, because there is so much attention that a newborn needs. I wanted to share the fun and the important memories with Nevalee. On January 31, 1996, our third blessing, Allie, arrived, our first daughter. I had promised my wife that we'd have boys *and* girls, so this made our family complete. *Whew.* Now I was off the hook!

Our joy was shared by my parents, and Papa Chuck was delighted to hear there would be another participant for the Sunday pancake tradition that I carried on—with his recipe—in my household.

By this time Dad's heart condition was getting worse. Although open-heart surgery had alleviated the problems for some years, it was now apparent that he was tiring much more easily. It wasn't a pronounced change, but I had so many decades of memories of his being hearty and strong that it was noticeable to me. Was this going to slow down his baseball appreciation? Not on your life. He had his satellite dish at home so that he wouldn't miss a single game during the year, and this year, as always, he was coming to Florida for spring training, as excited as ever, and getting ready for Opening Day—his favorite.

Mom preferred less travel, saying, "It's just as nice to watch it on television."

Dad, of course, thrived on the being there in the middle of the action, soaking up the ballpark ambience that watching on TV couldn't match. His capacity was undiminished for loving people and enjoying the chance to look around the stands, watching other fans and talking with them at length. So maybe he was supposed to have fewer hot dogs, so what? It was a change he'd *try* to accommodate.

Many changes were in the wind for the Yankees. George Steinbrenner had made a few important off-field moves to prepare for life without Don Mattingly, someone George really loved.

First, he hired Bob Watson as the general manager, who in turn hired Joe Torre as manager. The team was excited when we heard the news. Joe Torre had a fantastic reputation. Everybody who had ever played for Joe raved about him, both as a manager and as a person, remarking on how his clubhouse was relaxed and yet professional at the same time. While we all liked playing under Buck, Joe's approach of being a bit more hands-off was what we were ready for. Joe was known to be a player's manager who expected everyone to go out and give his all, while also allowing us to be ourselves—as long as his players were on the same page.

The Watson-Torre combination proved to be a stroke of genius when all was said and done. Another extraordinary change was the Yankees' new home away from home. George had built us Legends Field, in Tampa, the ultimate spring-training facility.

Maybe that's what baseball lore had in store for us. Maybe Ruth was looking down upon the house that he built and seeing a need to rekindle some of that old Bronx magic.

Legends Field gave us the spark. Its architecture made it look like something right out of history, out of the days of Ruth, façade and all. When Dad arrived in Florida, he marveled at how modern it was, yet how it seemed as if they'd miniaturized Yankee Stadium and brought it to Florida. The atmosphere was so enjoyable to him, almost as exciting as Opening Day, because of the fans, the intensity of the players, and the concessions. With his expert ear for the music of baseball, he also liked the fact that the park echoed the sounds of the game so well.

There were times during spring training, even though I had been playing for the Yankees for some time, when I thought, *God, I wish I weren't a line-drive hitter*. After the high of having three home runs in one game in the previous season, I'd find myself wishing I could hit the ball out of the park a little more often.

But I always returned, after a long face-to-face chat with Dad, to the fact that this was my strength and who I was—a line-drive hitter.

He'd look at me and give me his old refrain: "You hit the ball right on the button!" It still felt good hearing that from my father.

Dad also still wasn't afraid to let everyone in the stands know who his son was, and that embarrassed me to no end. He'd be talking up a storm with everyone in the sections nearby and telling them that I was his kid, the right fielder. No doubt that he had earned his bragging rights, though.

Legends Field was further indication to my father that George Steinbrenner had an incredible sense of Yankee history. Dad also liked George for the way he treated me. I may have been an adult now, thirty-three years old in February 1996, but I was still Chick O'Neill's son—his youngest at that.

When my dad first met George Steinbrenner at a Yankee game, George went out of his way to bring my father to come sit with him in his box, the owner's box. My father was blown away by this gesture, just like a little kid. He couldn't erase his grin of disbelief. The ultimate red-carpet treatment—getting to sit up in George Steinbrenner's box and watch a major-league baseball game. George always tried to make the ball-game experience a better one for Yankee players, their families, and the fans.

So we had a new spring-training facility, new managers, and a new team philosophy instilled in us by Joe Torre. It was the Torre way of doing things, a way that proved successful beyond anyone's wildest imagination.

Joe had an immediate calming affect on the team. He understood the ups and downs that a player goes through on the field, both offensively and defensively. He understood how to pace a season as a marathon rather than a sprint, how to magnify the positive and minimize the negative.

Moreover, there was an extra level of understanding within Joe that practically no other managers in the game possess. As an All-Star catcher with incredible numbers in his own right, he never forgot his ballplaying roots when he donned the manager's jacket and wrote out the starting-lineup cards.

A father figure and confidant to many players on the team, Joe wanted to be involved in our off-field affairs as a listening ear if we needed him. There is no one, in my opinion, who has played for him and who doesn't thank his lucky stars for that opportunity.

Though I never dreamed I would play for a manager who had so much in common with my father, it turned out that Joe Torre and Chick O'Neill shared many qualities. Both men were competitive yet supportive. Both were respectful of individuality on the team, while both commanded respect. Both believed that no one person is bigger than the team.

Both men also wanted their players to understand the "little ball" aspect of the game. They understood the nuances of baseball and how games could be won or lost based upon a mislaid bunt or a hit-and-run that was successful. Neither man was afraid to let everyone on the team know that bunting, and doing the little things, is what wins games. Both embraced the importance of fundamentals.

Joe was focused on proper baserunning, just like Dad, and the need for speed and sacrificing runners over, as well as the need for base stealing. Both men knew the game inside and out, and both saw the game from outside and between the lines with the deepest of perception. They knew that everyone on the team is an individual, with his own needs, problems, and worries.

With such similarities, it was a naturally comfortable situation for me to thrive as part of Joe Torre's Yankees. And when I didn't play well, I felt that much worse about letting my teammates down—and letting Joe down. It wasn't about me. It was about my teammates, the coaches, the manager, and the owner. My admiration and respect for Joe Torre made me even harder on myself, both at the plate and on the field.

Part of what made him so motivational is that he did not pressure his players. Only a ballplayer knows the true compliment behind this remark. Joe let you as a player go out and play your game. With Joe Torre you gave 100 percent, not 78 percent, and whatever worked for you to get to that 100 percent mark was fine with him.

Maybe that was why, rather than trying to lessen my intensity, he appreciated how deeply I cared. If my less-than-best performance had contributed to a loss, I would actually feel I'd let down Joe and Tino Martinez and the rest of my teammates. Obviously, I'd never lost that part of me that had been my own worst critic since childhood.

My outbursts, however, must have made Joe insane at times. He didn't yell at me, but he did flash me some worried looks when I'd punch a watercooler, like he was thinking, *Paul's going to break his hand*.

Then again, he knew that was how I was and didn't try to change me. That's how perceptive he was about human nature, mine for sure. We also could talk about things in general, off the subject of baseball. We joked and talked about my family, about growing up in Ohio.

Sometimes the best manager is the one who lets the players bond together as a team and then joins in that bond with the players, as Joe did with us. A physically rugged man who can speak softly yet who has great authority, Joe earned my further admiration for his tenacity as a survivor when, over time, he dealt with his own life-threatening bout with prostate cancer and his concerns over his brother Frank's health problems.

Joe Torre also expressed a strong sense of the impact athletes have on kids around the country, and he always emphasized the ideals of good sportsmanship and family values. His belief that kids were watching major-league baseball and taking their cues from our behavior was right on.

You don't win three World Championships in a row without teamwork. In 1996 we didn't know we were building toward having the dynasty that we would have, but we knew we had a special group of guys that could win a game at any time.

We played every game as a team. It was the Yankee way of playing ball, the reason I felt so fortunate that my journey had brought me along to be part of this great ride. So many elements have to come together for a team to be a dynasty, and I was about to witness them firsthand.

Besides teamwork, we did the little things. It was old-school baseball. We kept the same nucleus together, and that's what made the run so special. I think, as the years go by, that the team will be written about as a special team at a special time in a special city, mainly because of Joe Torre, to me the greatest manager ever, and his influence on our team.

In early 1996 that was all in the future, but I quickly realized that Joe was to be a pivotal force in my career and my life, as a member of my true extended family. So, too, I soon saw, would coach Don Zimmer, who likewise became family.

Zimmer and the other coaches who came on board at this time were a direct reflection of the personality of our manager. Zim, a real character who'd been around for many eras of baseball, had a great way of making me laugh when I was being hard on myself. He used to kid me every time I beat myself up or trashed a watercooler or a batting helmet, saying, "If you want to quit, I know a bricklaying company back in Columbus." He went on to rub it in, saying they'd hire me because they needed someone with my tenacity.

On the first day of spring training, when I met Don Zimmer, I had no idea what humor lurked inside of him. He was a "get your glove and let's go play" type person. But that went hand in hand with the professional code of conduct and the winning attitude that was being set in tone, and Zim did a fantastic job of making us all focus in on winning a championship.

It didn't take long for his zingers to start flying. He was also a storehouse of baseball knowledge and anecdotes. Plus, Zim thrived on taking chances, whether it was baserunning chances or betting on the horses.

One time with the Cubs, he told me, he put the hit-and-run play on with bases loaded! You can't do stuff like that, but he did. That's Zim, true to form. He was so vociferous during games, he made up our own cheering section in the dugout—always jumping up out of his seat and yelling at a big hit.

It was also Don Zimmer and company who introduced me to the intriguing game of bridge. We started out playing at the stadium during a rain delay, and Joe Girardi, John Wetteland, and Zim taught me how to play.

We played what we called "Yankees Bridge." The basic format in bridge is that you play by points, and you can ask your partner to help you out. Naturally, we had some of our own rules that let us kind of cheat.

One day that went a bit too far, when Kenny Rodgers was Zimmer's partner and turned to him, saying, "Zim, I'm a little short." Kenny wasn't kidding. He had no points at all! Of course, this went beyond breaking a rule; it meant you were done.

Zim stared back with a blank look, as if someone had hit him over the head. The expression on his face was priceless. Zim was being destroyed in the game by Kenny—and they were partners!

It was hard for me not to crack a smile. When I did, I knew Zim wouldn't let me hear the end of it.

Don Zimmer really had the right touch, using his sense of humor with me when I was venting my frustration for a lousy at-bat by punching an unassuming watercooler or kicking an innocent batting helmet. Otherwise not much of a fuss was ever really made, until one day that year when general manager Bob Watson called me into his office and laid down the law.

"Paul," Bob began, a somber look on his face, "the Yankees organization is concerned about these . . . ." His voice trailed off as he searched for the right word. What he really meant, he continued, was that it was felt I needed to curb my intensity.

Suppressing a grin, I was laughing inside, relieved that this had nothing to do with the caliber of my playing.

But Bob went further, spelling it out for me quite plainly. "The thing is, if you break your hand because you hit a watercooler, it might affect your contract."

Of course, I told him that I'd do my best not to endanger myself, and then I left his office, still somewhat bemused but resolved to have quieter, gentler outbursts. He had definitely made his point.

There are not enough pages in one book for me to properly sing the praises of my Yankee teammates. They were simply stellar ballplayers and the greatest friends on and off the field.

One of my closest friendships was with Bernie Williams. Soft-spoken and quiet, he remained that way throughout his rise to superstardom and multiple All-Star teams—the same down-to-earth, everyday person he had been when he moved up to the majors the previous year.

Because the right fielder and the center fielder work in tandem in the outfield, there is an important connection the two must have. He and I had that great connection, a way of communicating without words. Our bond was not made on paper but forged in grass and lumber. If ever I hit a wall reaching for the ball to get that extra out, Bernie was instantly there to back me up. If I missed a chance to get on base—kicking myself on the way back to the dugout—before I took my seat, Bernie was driving in the run.

As much as he laughed at me for my pregame intensity, I laughed out of disbelief at how relaxed he was before a game. While I was pacing back and forth, Bernie was asleep on the couch half an hour before the game started. That was his way of relaxing. The first at-bat, he'd calmly walk up and hit a home run.

Bernie and I also connected in our love for music. We each played instruments—Bernie the classical guitar, me still keeping up my drum playing. Whenever we could, he and I had jam sessions in the paint room that was tucked away in the labyrinth of Yankee Stadium.

I agreed with Bernie's view on the intersection of music and baseball which, he commented, were alike in that "you only have one shot to get it right."

When you get up to that plate, that's it. Likewise, when you're performing as a musician, it's not a rehearsal—you've got your one opportunity to perform brilliantly, and if you mess it up, it's lost forever.

His philosophy echoed the words someone wise once said: You only remember the World Series winners, not the teams who lost.

Catcher Joe Girardi—who came to the Yankees in 1996—was another awesome player and a very close friend. A wonderful father and person, he and I were both ardent fans of great Italian cooking and enjoyed taking our wives out for superb dinners at Mulino's up in White Plains.

Whenever the team was gearing up for playoffs, Joe and I had a preplayoff routine that began at Mulino's, allowing us to take in some Italian food, click glasses in a toast, and get our minds set for the battles ahead.

Joe and I even ordered the same dish, but not by design—risotto with red sauce and chicken. *Delizioso.* Mulino's had the best bread, cheese, and olive oil—everything I couldn't get in Cincinnati.

The best Italian food in the United States was another joy I'd discovered as a transplant to New York. The red sauces, unlike any I'd had before, tasted like they came right out of a kitchen in Italy.

Joe Girardi could eat with the greatest eaters of all time. I thought he had a tapeworm. He could eat and eat and eat. Long after I put down my fork and couldn't manage another bite, he was still at it, making me wonder, *Man, where is all that food going?*

First baseman Tino Martinez was another table setter who really contributed big time for the team. Temperament-wise, I think that Tino and I were both wired the same way. I *knew* how he felt after a poor game, and he *knew* how I felt after a poor game. Bernie and Derek Jeter could deal with an 0-for-5 day because they knew they were getting five hits the next day.

If Tino or I had a bad game, we'd take that game with us right into the clubhouse and right to the dinner table. It never left us. We'd sit there at our lockers and shake our heads and ask ourselves if this poor day would turn into a terrible week, or even a terrible month.

Thankfully, Tino and I also turned our intensity into making things happen in the following games.

Another guy known for his intensity was Andy Pettitte, who in 1996 had a terrific year, going 21–8. On the mound Andy was formidable—so intimidating with his terrifying stare and the bill of his cap down low over his eyes. I liked his confidence at such a young age, and I liked how he carried himself with such poise. Andy also was a listener. He took instruction from the veteran pitchers and really excelled.

Scary though he was when pitching, off the field he was a role model as an exemplary human being and great father. Andy lived next door to us, and our kids played together. We used to drive to the ballpark together. A Texas boy, he'd grown up hunting and was eager for me to go out in the off-season with him and share his hunting enthusiasm. Much as I liked his company and was willing to try most sports, I could never see myself out in the woods walking around with a rifle.

Andy's drawl and down-home talk were a source of amusement for my kids, who'd never heard some of his southern expressions back in Ohio—phrases like "Fixin' to go to dinner" and "How y'all doin'?"

"That's not in my English book. Where'd that come from?" they'd ask me.

It appeared that 1996 was "fixin'" to be a magical year for the Yankees—for all kinds of reasons. Whatever they were, this year *it* all happened. This season was our date with destiny, the first of many such glory years in the Bronx.

Two standouts in the regular season came early. The first occurred on April 30 in Baltimore. As a gritty team that never liked to lose, the Yankees held forth even as the clock kept on ticking in a game against the Orioles that felt endless. We walked away when it finally did end with a 13–10 win, doing so after four hours and twenty-one minutes, the longest nine-inning game in major-league baseball history. (The record we broke was four hours, eighteen minutes for a 1962 Dodgers–Giants game.)

Then, on May 14 in Yankee Stadium, against Lou Piniella's Seattle Mariners, Dwight Gooden had a game for the history books. Doc was always a big-game pitcher, but this one was different. He was a Yankee now, not a Met, and he had been down some difficult roads in recent years. He was also not the same pitcher he'd been when he first came into the major leagues and blew guys away with his fastball.

But that night he was on fire and pitched a breathtaking no-hitter, giving us a 2–0 victory, throwing only the eighth regular-season no-hitter in Yankee history.

Gerald Williams proved crucial in this game by snatching a four-hundred-foot Alex Rodriguez liner in the first inning. With the combination of Doc's spectacular pitching, Gerald's play, and a strong effort on the part of the rest of the team, it was cause for celebration for us all. And it was fitting that the game happened at the beginning of Joe's tenure with the Yankees.

Dad had the excitement of watching Dwight's no-hitter, thanks to his satellite dish, which had him glued to the TV. About his biggest frustration in life was the nights when the signal was blocked because of FCC rules.

On those nights, Nevalee would call him at home and give him a play-by-play description of the game as it was unfolding. She was happy to do it, knowing how this really got him going and made up somewhat for his not being there in person.

This was the time period that I went 235 games (1995–96) without an error, definitely something to feel good about for a perfectionist like me.

As the regular season drew to a close and we made it into the playoffs against the Orioles, Dad started making plans to come east. These were games he had to be there in person to witness.

Yankee fever was starting to burn. We knew we had a chance to go all the way. But we also knew that until we beat the Orioles, the World Series would always be a goal unattained.

The excitement brewing in the streets of Manhattan was increasingly noticeable. Up until this year, I had not spent much time venturing out of our sheltered life in Rye, but this season we'd been making a point of trying to take more advantage of all that the city had to offer.

In the first week of October, New York City was in its autumn colors—the navy and white of Yankee caps and sweatshirts on fans everywhere I went. This was the first time outside the ballpark that I felt, just walking around, how much the team meant to New York. They wore their colors, talking baseball as they moved along in pairs and groups or stopped to buy food from street vendors who set their radio dials to WFAN, the sports-talk radio station, all day long.

The passion was different from the feeling anywhere else I'd been, totally different from Cincinnati. Reds fans were devoted, I realized, but they didn't go near the extremes of the Yankee fans.

We got off to a great start winning Game One of the ALCS, then losing Game Two to Baltimore. In the eighth inning of Game Three, we came from behind for the win, then followed with a win in Game Four.

After we'd cleared that hurdle, our confidence was riding high. The fans fueled our fervor even more, and in Game Four, I was able to contribute with a home run in an 8–4 win. Dad and Mom were there for that happy moment, as was Nevalee, the three down in front cheering as I made my run of the bases, rounded third, and trotted home.

"We're going to the World Series again!" I said jubilantly to Nevalee in the dugout tunnel after the game. There in Baltimore we had just clinched the American League Championship Series 4–1, an emotional release for the whole team and an unbelievable feeling of accomplishment, knowing that we had passed the last obstacle to getting into the World Series.

What moved me more than anything was seeing Joe Torre's reaction—his pride a true sight to behold. Although sometimes a stoic, he allowed himself to be very emotional this night. That's when the significance of our coming this far—his first year with the Yankees—sank in for me. It wasn't just what he had achieved so far with us. These were the fruits of his labor during an entire ballplaying career, years of managing well, and his first opportunity to do something like this. All of us were doubly inspired—players, coaches, fans, and the media.

New York was ready for the World Series and everyone seemed to be singing, "Who's afraid of the big, bad Atlanta Braves?"

The Braves had won the NLCS after a scorching back-and-forth seven-game series against the St. Louis Cardinals. If we had any thoughts that they might not have the juice for Game One at Yankee Stadium, we were sadly mistaken.

The Ohio O'Neill cheering section was on hand—with Dad eating his hot dog (which by now the doctors had forbidden), Mom looking the other way, and my brothers Mike and Pat, who had come up with them. In a throwback to childhood and other times when I put too much pressure on myself to impress family and friends, I didn't have my best showing after becoming too preoccupied with not wanting to hear Mike and Pat tell me after the game that I had stunk.

It wasn't just me. The Braves trounced us in the Bronx, winning 12–1. Dad's encouraging motto—"Just go get 'em tomorrow night!"—was not brought to bear when the Braves returned to shut us out 4–0 in Game Two.

Now we had to go to Atlanta down two games. Mike was of the opinion, so he insisted to Pat—an optimist like Dad—that we had blown our chances by losing both games in the Bronx. Pat, however, never lost hope. Later I had the pleasure of messing with Mike for concluding that we were finished after the first two games, reminding him that he'd given up on us.

Though anything could happen, the tension was building as the team flew to Atlanta. I was not thinking about "coming back" per se. I was thinking merely about winning Game Three. The way to win, we knew in our hearts, was to play to win every game, and for me that meant wanting to hit in every inning and connect with every pitch.

That was exactly the Yankee baseball way of playing, which allowed us to beat the Braves in Atlanta in Game Three. But they returned in Game Four ready to resume their momentum, pushing the game into a tenth inning, when we found ourselves behind with only a small hope of pulling something out of the hat. And then, in the blink of an eye, Jim Leyritz transformed our fate with a monster home run—the turning point in our baseball lives as Yankee players.

For years to come after this home run, whenever we were down, somehow things magically worked themselves out and just seemed to click and happen for us. We had proven to ourselves that we had the mettle to come back and win.

With the win of Games Three and Four, we also showed the world that the Atlanta bullpen was human. It was our time to make some noise. Toward the end of Game Five, with the Yankees leading barely, 1–0, I was able show a little leather myself with a catch to take a hit away from Luis Polonia—ending the game in victory. The cool calm of being in the zone for that play was followed by a delayed panic reaction I experienced while running back all the way into the infield. *Oh, my God,* I thought, *this is the World Series! What if I hadn't caught that ball?*

Andy Pettitte had put on some remarkable performances and solidified his place in baseball history in my book as one of the best postseason pitchers. His mastery made Game Five an unbelievable game to witness and to play in, one of the best postseason games I've ever been privileged to experience in my major-league career.

Joe Torre later admitted that after we lost the first two games, he actually told George Steinbrenner, "Oh, don't worry. We'll get swept at home, but we'll go down there and sweep them to come back and win it at home."

After we won Game Five on Braves' home soil, it appeared that fate was following Joe's prediction.

Returning to Yankee Stadium for Games Six and Seven—if a seventh game was necessary—we believed that the momentum had now swung in the Yankees' favor.

Dad's optimism that we would probably win Game Six and not need a last game was buoyed even higher when he felt the energy that vibrated throughout the stands. He had gotten to be a part of the 1990 World Series triumph when I was with the Reds, but he could feel that this place was different from Cincinnati. It was a joy to know that he was out there in the crowd, taking it in, really sensing just how deep the passion ran in the stands.

The night belonged to the Yankees and, with our 3–2 win at the end of the game, so, too, did the 1996 World Series—culminating with a celebration pileup on the field that I jumped onto last! Back in the locker room, still in a state of ecstatic delirium, I felt just a tinge of disappointment that my son Andy wasn't there to share in the celebration. At seven years old, he would have really enjoyed watching us win, although at this late hour he was probably best off where he was—at home in bed, fast asleep.

Then, as if this fairy tale just had to get even better, all of a sudden I turned around and there was Andy—right behind me!

Seeing his beaming smile and twinkling eyes brought tears into my own. Nevalee had brought him to the game after all. She didn't want him to miss out on the historic win. It was such an unexpected treat—having my little guy walk over to me and seeing the fun my teammates had with him.

For a moment I flashed back to a November day in 1992 when my future had seemed so bleak after hearing the news that I'd been traded to the Yankees and my father had treated it like the best thing that could have happened. He had been right about everything. Three baseball seasons later, my wildest dreams had been surpassed. I had a World Series win in New York, and I was sharing it with my father and my son.

The intergenerational love of baseball was in evidence when the mayor of fair Gotham City, Rudy Giuliani, pulled out all the stops for a World Series victory parade through the Canyon of Heroes. Born and bred a Yankee fan, Mayor Giuliani was so genuine in his love for the team that, mayor or not, he wasn't going to pretend to be impartial—he was going to root for his Yankees just as he had all his life.

When the Reds won the World Series in 1990, there was a parade in Cincinnati that a few thousand fans attended. In 1996, New York City saw 3.5 million faithful attend our ticker-tape parade. The victory was truly collective—it belonged to the fans, to the team, to the management, and to the city itself.

Joe Torre deserved the loudest cheers of all. He had been through so much this season, with the health battles of his brother Frank, who, thank God, was recovering in dramatic fashion.

The parade that year opened my eyes to the torch of Yankee pride that was being passed from one generation to the next.

Fathers (and mothers, too) really did teach it to their children, who in turn taught it to their kids. My teammates seemed as much in awe of this show of love as I did. We knew, of course, that the Yankee fans were the best, but to see more than 3 million people cheering their hearts out for you with all their loyalty and their "Yankees Passion" is humbling, unbelievable, and wonderful.

As a player you don't realize how special a season will be until it's all over. It's like the perfect rose that you've cultivated, clipped, and given away to that sweetheart of yours. You don't know how beautiful and special it is until you get the smile in return.

The smile we got from New York City and the fans' devotion made me want even more to do well so as not to let these faithful supporters down. If we had known of the extent to which the fans loved us before the Series, I remarked to Nevalee, I would have personally been a nervous wreck.

Many fans, thankfully, loved Yankee baseball for all the tradition and the ambience, just one big carnival atmosphere filled with fun, laughter, food, and excitement, and whoever won didn't really matter as much.

Although, as has been said before, nothin' beats winning!

The 1997 season seemed limitless to us when we took to Legends Field for spring training. How could we top ourselves? Another World Series win quickly came to mind.

Interestingly, we started very slowly out of the gate that year but then began to pick up steam along the way. On June 6 we won one of the hardest-fought games in our history, fifteen innings against the Red Sox, beating them 11–5.

The season saw Mariano Rivera rack up 43 saves, and Mike Stanton and Jeff Nelson had terrific seasons as setup men for Mariano. Mo Rivera now had the closing role passed on to him after Wetteland—who had been incredible during the last World Series—moved on to join the Texas Rangers.

On September 5 in Yankee Stadium, we once again played a historically long game with our rival Baltimore Orioles. The game took four hours and twenty-two minutes to play, the longest nine-inning game in major-league history to date, breaking the previous record we had set one year before when we beat the Orioles.

Ironically, we lost the game, forcing us to give up ownership of a record. But, in the grand scheme of things, it did little to dampen our spirits. And by the time we finished the season, we found ourselves in first place.

When we arrived in Cleveland for the AL divisional playoffs, the Indians' fans were pumped and partyin', ready to get us out of the way as their big obstacle to the ALCS and the World Series. We knew that the five-game series would be tight, but we also knew that we could win.

We won the first game, lost the second, and then I was able to help in a big way for a win in Game Three with a grand slam in the fourth inning. We looked to take the fourth game, but a last-minute rally by the Indians gave them the win. We played Game Five like the 1996 World Champions that we were, and thought we had it in the bag until Cleveland's Roberto Alomar brought about a reversal of fortune with a home run. In the top of the ninth, when we were down by a run, I hit a double and made it to second with a very unconventional slide, but it wasn't enough.

Suddenly we were out of it. We had come up short. The Yankees had shown a lot of heart, although it didn't make losing any easier on my stomach. As a matter of fact, that was one of the most bitter losses I have ever experienced.

The plane ride seemed to take forever. None of the things we had done right or the stirring victories of the season that had led up to this loss mattered on that morose flight back to New York.

We arrived home in the early-morning hours. Soon after that we were telling one another, "See you next year in Tampa."

I was as disappointed as I had ever been in baseball in my life. The idea of having to be home to watch the World Series bothered me so much that I refused to turn on the television when Cleveland went on to play against the Florida Marlins.

This was practically breaking an O'Neill family commandment— "Thou shalt watch the World Series from beginning to end"—a tradition I had excitedly upheld since the age of ten. Finally, after my own O'Neill kids let me know how badly they wanted to watch the games, I tuned in to Game Seven and allowed myself to watch, only because the Marlins were having a miracle run.

The Marlins went on to win in extra innings on a crucial hit in the bottom of the tenth inning, a walk-off World Series win at home for the Marlins. But the Florida Cinderella story that gave them their World Series victory turned out to have a sad postscript when the team was suddenly dismantled just weeks later, an ugly showing for major-league baseball.

The off-season passed more slowly than it had in a while, my disappointment about losing to Cleveland gnawing at me long into December. In my heart of hearts, I knew we were the better team, and I still feel that way today.

And then it was a new year, a new season. Almost on the dot, when the calendar page turned to January, I was suddenly reenergized. Something kicked in that Dad had long tried to impress upon me in times of crisis—that the secret to baseball success was being able to learn from failure and move on. In fact, the notion that we had even failed the year before was overshadowed by the idea that we could use what we'd learned to power us through the coming season.

February couldn't get here fast enough for me. We were Joe Torre's New York Yankees, and we had unfinished business awaiting us.

NINE

The Record Year—125 Wins

With that shift in attitude, it seemed to me that spring training arrived before I could blink an eye, and there I was in my batting-practice jersey standing in Legends Field with my teammates—the 1998 season ahead of us. In the locker room, there was a marked sense of renewed determination in the air and in the whole team's demeanor.

Hopes ride high every season at spring training, because there's a fresh year in front of you, a clean slate, a chance to hit .300, win the division, the World Series. *Again!*

In spite of all the good feeling and optimism, there was a glaring absence at Legends Field this year—that of Chick O'Neill. Battling coronary artery disease was taking its toll on my father. He was seventy-eight years old and, though he was mentally as spry as ever, his stamina had diminished and it was hard for him to perform the daily activities that had once made life so enjoyable. When I visited him before coming to Tampa, I'd tried to keep a stiff upper lip and tell myself that he would be fine, but seeing him in a weakened condition just broke my heart.

Dad was as upbeat as ever, promising me that he was going on at least one road trip this year, not wanting to miss his now familiar stomping grounds at Fenway Park, if not make it to other games as well.

We kept in touch even more closely by phone, if that was possible, with me checking in for his perennial pep talks and congratulations— depending on the situation.

In April I benefited from his "keep the faith" attitude, because I had a month without one home run, one of the few times in my career that had ever happened to me. But in May, to Dad's jubilation, I drove in a career-high 33 runs. I had also never done this in one month. That same month I collected my 1,500th career hit on May 22 at Fenway Park.

Five days earlier had come one of the most memorable games of 1998, when we played against the Minnesota Twins. As it so happened, this day game was being dubbed "Beanie Baby Day" at Yankee Sta- dium, and the park was filled with kids eager to get the Beanie Babies that were being given away. No one needed to tell me how hot these toys were—they had swept the country, with girls and boys collecting the officially branded little stuffed animals. I had my own assignment from home: bring home a Beanie Baby for each of my kids.

Probably most people in the park that overcast Bronx day were there for these collectibles, and the game was secondary to them. That is, until the late innings. This was when the entire sellout crowd of fifty-six thousand realized that magic was in the air, and it was not coming from their kids' toys. It was emanating from the pitcher's mound, where David Wells was pitching his way into baseball history.

By the sixth inning, Wells had so far pitched a perfect game, and wanting to make it happen for him, we started to get nervous, hoping that any of the high fly balls didn't get caught in the hazy air and make us miss the play. The last thing any teammate wants is to ruin a pitcher's perfect game with an error or to misjudge a ball and have it end up being a hit instead of an out.

A pitcher rarely gets the opportunity to toss a no-hitter, much less a perfect game, and there hadn't been one at Yankee Stadium since Don Larsen had his magical stuff back in the 1956 World Series. No doubt, a lot of history had happened to this team in forty-two years.

All of that was in our thoughts when we took to the dugout. The epitome of empathetic nervousness was fellow pitcher David Cone, who was caught on camera with his sunglasses down over his eyes, slouched into his jacket that covered up most of his face so all that could be seen were his dark shades.

In the top of the seventh inning, I ran out to right field to take my position, waiting for the next Minnesota batter, thinking, *Hit the ball to me, but make it an easy play! No sinking line drives, please!*

Earlier in the game, I'd felt that Wells had something special going, and in this inning I started counting down the outs. All players who are part of a once-in-a-lifetime occurrence like this start doing the mental math as the clock winds down.

I had the pleasure of making a catch in the ninth to end it, and Wells had his perfect game. Just as I punched my fist in the air, David pumped his fist in the air at the mound.

We were overjoyed celebrating with David Wells. The fans were in shock. They had come to the park that day to get their Beanie Baby toy, and now they'd witnessed baseball history.

"Boomer" Wells—my Yankee teammate who loved heavy metal, the Metallica-type music I'd personally rather hear in the clubhouse than music that puts me to sleep—was now Mr. Perfect. He showed me over the years that he was a big-game pitcher with a lot of passion when it came to his teammates. David cared about every game and how his fellow Yankees fared in all of our games, not just those in which he was involved.

David presented each of us with game rings as a symbol of his appreciation—a gesture that really touched me. He could have claimed the glory as his alone, yet he took the time to say to us with these rings, *Hey, thanks, I wanted you guys to know that you were a part of this historic day.*

It's for reasons like this that I say David Wells could play on my team any day of the week.

That perfect game was good luck for me, because I had a seventeen-game hitting streak from May 24 to June 10, batting .400 during that stretch. I was totally locked in, and the ball seemed to be the size of a grapefruit. I also made the 1998 All-Star Team, an experience that was always a thrill, both for the honor of being in such fine company and because of how much I had loved watching these games as a kid.

Plus, it was one more tribute to share with my father—who kept reassuring me in our conversations that he would see me at Fenway soon.

For a handful of different reasons, 1998 was the year that the Yankees became media stars, with many of us players making entertainment and society gossip sections as regularly as we were getting sports coverage.

Not only that, more than ever before, other media and sports celebrities were making frequent appearances in the company of Yankees. As a huge fan of Monica Seles, I found it a kick when she came out to take batting practice with us. To my surprise, she proceeded to whiff at every ball pitched to her, even when the pitcher moved up and stood about ten feet away from her. With her power during her legendary tennis career, I had expected her to knock the ball right out of the park. Just goes to show, everything's relative. After all, I couldn't return a tennis serve from Seles!

One of the nicest perks of meeting celebrities in the sports and entertainment fields was getting to meet some of my favorite musicians. At a John Mellencamp New Year's Eve concert, I had the pleasure of going backstage during intermission to meet John.

So here's the kicker: I'm standing backstage with John Mellencamp, and we're making small talk, and out of nowhere he says, "Hey, Paul, you're going to play the encore tonight."

I say something really brilliant, like "Yeah, right!"

He just repeats himself before walking away, "You're going to play the encore tonight." Then he turns back to tell me the song—"Gloria."

He was serious. When he called me up to the stage to sit down at the drums, I had no choice but just to go for it, and the crowd, loving the novelty of seeing a major-leaguer rock out, pumped me up even more.

What a blast! I'm so glad he forced me out onstage. To this day I can hardly believe that was me playing with him and his band on New Year's Eve. Thank God, I've got photographs to prove it!

My other adventure into music-related fame took place during the 1998 season, when Madison Square Garden Television decided to produce a commercial that would boast Bernie Williams on his electric guitar and me on the drums.

It sounded cool until we arrived at the studio and opened up the door where MSG was taping the piece.

There it was: the drum set . . . a *tiny* drum set!

I stared at it in utter disbelief. It had to be a little kid's toy drum set. Turning to Bernie, I didn't know whether to laugh or cry. *Man,* I was thinking, *how embarrassing.* People were going to think it was *my* drum set.

And they did, or so I've been told. When I think about how nice my drums are at home and how I actually played something on this toy set on television, it's hysterical. Bernie and I thought they'd have some top-of-the-line monster drum set for me. My drum set at home was pretty awesome; they could have used it. Of course, I couldn't do much more on it than I could on that mini set, but at least it looked great!

The commercial added to the publicity surge.

Getting so much attention was a strange phenomenon to me. On the plus side, it was wonderful to think that ten-year-old boys watching us play in 1998 would be twenty years old someday and remember the starting lineup of our team. The continuity of the team's lineup—which the Yankees had been developing—made for a lasting impression in the minds of children across the country.

That thought was prominent in my mind when the Toms River, New Jersey, team won the Little League World Series and the Yankees toasted them as our two teams took the field together. Each player on our club stood beside the Toms River player of our respective position during the singing of the national anthem at Yankee Stadium before a capacity crowd. The Little League champion right fielder who stood beside me had such a great smile on his face, it took me way back to my own Little League days and simply made me happy to see him so elated.

In my mind's eye, I was remembering other events that brought smiles to my face when I was his age—my childhood with my dad at the ballpark, our trip to Crosley Field when I watched Clemente guarding right field. I could still see Pirates number 21 planted in the outfield, poised to catch a ball, then plucking it out of the air and rifling a shot to home to throw the runner out! How could you not love a guy like that if you're a seven-year-old kid? And then I flashed on that Roberto Clemente autograph Dad had forged for me with love.

The ten-year-old at my side was probably a younger version of me. Would he and his teammates remember this moment of their own achievement and getting to meet the 1998 Yankees as fondly as I did the moments in my past? My guess was that some of them would be remembering this day in a major-league ballpark somewhere down the line.

Congratulating the kids one by one in the dugout, I wondered if there was a dad in the group who would be taking them to a Dairy Queen.

The media attention from such events was fine, although I had mixed feelings about the fact that I was receiving an inordinate amount of publicity. In general, I was media-shy and had long avoided putting myself in the limelight or running to the microphones. But at one juncture, when I thought that I'd hit a streak of bad baseball luck, I got it into my head that Yankees sports announcer Michael Kay could change my luck by interviewing me on his radio show. Sure enough, I did the interview and had a great game. After that, in the playoffs, he interviewed me every day, and we kept winning!

Michael Kay is a player's announcer. Not only does he know the game, but he is a huge Yankees fan—which made the experience all the sweeter. Plus, I became so comfortable talking on air about the game I knew and loved that sports analysis was to become an important interest for me.

A lot was being made humorously of my baseball idiosyncrasies. My ongoing batting practice in right field received a great amount of attention, and ribbing from opposing players. "What is that, tai chi?" a couple of them asked me.

When Mike Mussina came over to the Yankees from Baltimore, he laughingly confessed that the Orioles had made a game of trying to predict how many times I'd practice my batting stance and swing in right field after an inning. It became a running joke on their bench.

Some of Don Zimmer's poking fun of my quirks also filtered into the public domain. More than once, when I was upset with myself in the dugout, Zim pulled me aside to tell me—and the reporters around us—that he could help me out. He had the perfect solution to my outbursts with the watercoolers. This was our bit.

Just to get him going, I'd get into it, saying, "Zim, I've had enough of this! I'm going home. That's it."

"Paul, I've got a friend who owns a construction company in Columbus," Zim would tell me.

I knew where this was headed, as usual. I'd just shake my head and laugh.

"Well, I've got that buddy in Cincinnati if you need a job," he'd rub it in with his own burst of laughter.

There is a sort of sacred relationship between a player and manager, and a fine line between joking around and being serious. There is no such line with a coach, especially with Don Zimmer. So it worked out that I joked around with Joe through Zim. Laughter as the best medicine was Zim's Rx, and I had more fun with him than with any coach I've known.

When it came to my ritual of getting the mud out of my cleats by knocking it off with a bang of the bat against my foot, even Zim was rendered speechless. He winced as he looked at the chunks taken out of my bats, shook his head, and put his hands to his eyes, laughing. I shrugged in response. After all, the bats may have paid the price when it came to aesthetics, but they usually did the job for me whenever I stepped inside that chalk-lined box.

Publicity continued to focus this year on my emotional intensity and the trail of wounded watercoolers left in its wake. My teammates kidded me about my tantrums throughout all of 1998, because, as the team won, we made the papers more frequently, as did my frustrated reactions about giving away any at-bats, even though I was hitting over .300 the entire season.

· At one really inopportune moment, I absolutely went crazy during a game, and this time my fit occurred in the bathroom inside the dugout tunnel. It was supposedly out of view of everyone, but for some reason one of the Madison Square Garden cameras got an angle view of me inside the dugout. To my horror, MSG had a feed that broadcast my fit live, capturing it on tape for millions of viewers around the world.

My wife told me the very next day that our kids had seen it, as well as all their friends, and that they were talking about it at their Little League game. Nevalee was justifiably upset with me, while I felt remorseful that they had seen my ugly display and, worse, that it had happened at all.

From then on I attempted to turn over a new leaf and tried to subdue my reactions, at least to keep them away from the cameras as much as possible. Not that I never felt like I wanted to kick a watercooler again! My concern was that I not give a misimpression to kids that I was crazed. In reality, the watercooler was like a punching bag that allowed me to vent naturally pent-up feelings and expressions of my own displeasure with myself.

Finding oneself under public scrutiny, it is easy to feel misunderstood or to react defensively by having the media build stories that are out of proportion to the truth. There's a saying for most celebrities:

"Don't explain, don't complain." That's why I didn't combat portrayals of me that may have been exaggerated, or not. The fact is, however, there was a certain healthy outlet that let me get something off of my back so I could go on with the game, rather than holding it inside and getting me an ulcer. Striking out with a man on third base was enough of a weight, and I didn't need any more baggage, so when I vented, it was a release for me, letting me start clean for the rest of the game.

My fellow Yankees, I believe, understood me well and knew that if I had a bad day, I saw it as *my* fault, not theirs. I always made it clear that I was upset with me, not with anyone else—and I hope the public understood that in the end—but I was never mad at my teammates or at reporters. The media had their jobs in front of them. They had to ask me the tough questions, and I wanted to oblige them by answering.

Reporters don't make mistakes in the outfield or at the plate, ballplayers do, and the players should be adult enough to answer questions and take responsibility for their actions by addressing the media after the game.

While I took my lumps and became more image-conscious, I did a lot of soul-searching to get to the bottom of why I had never been able to stop being hard on myself. Ultimately, the answer came that those outbursts were a product of the way I was wired. Dad was wired differently, with his ability to infuse his passion with his undying optimism. What I'd have wished to have had that quality, but I didn't.

Could a tiger change his stripes? That I wasn't sure about, but the responsibilities that came with the turf of being a professional athlete in the public eye were something I couldn't take lightly. I looked in the mirror one day and asked myself if this was a trait I wanted to pass on to my younger fans, and I quickly thought the better of it. My decision was to try harder to curb my public displays of anger, while I knew I could never curb my intensity for the game.

In my heart I knew who I was as a person, and as a husband and father. What was more, so did my own children, who had never copied my behavior before, and who laughed off the MSG incident.

But then came an event that really reinforced my need to lighten up. Not long after the hubbub had settled down, I came home from the ballpark and was greeted by Nevalee with a sober expression on her face. "Andy is pretty upset," she said without further explanation.

When I went to find my nine-year-old, I was concerned to see him sitting by himself with his head down, slumped over as if in a state of total dejection.

Going to him and reaching to touch his shoulder, I asked, "What's up, Andy? You okay, pal?"

Andy looked up at me, shrugged his shoulders, and shook his head, exhaling a heavy sigh, finally explaining, "I gave away some at-bats today."

"Oh, my God, Andy . . . ," I began, and then my voice trailed off as I searched for the right words.

What had I done? For me to say something along those lines to Tino Martinez was one thing. To hear those words coming from my own son was terrifying!

Was that a double standard? Of course, I'd been saying it since I was young, and the cardinal rule in baseball is, don't give away at-bats. But I didn't want my son growing up to put the kind of pressure on himself that had plagued me for too long. If he turned out to be hardwired that way, so be it. But in the meantime I wanted him to have fun out there and to love baseball for the joy of playing it.

Thinking of Dad, I tried to use all his best lines on my own son, reminding Andy of the terrific hits and plays he'd made in the past, encouraging him just to go out and hit the ball right on the button the next time.

Later I sat down for a serious talk with Nevalee, aware that, despite the irony, this wasn't a laughing matter. "I can't believe it," I said to her. "This is Little League, and he's acting like me!"

My wife gave me a knowing look that was enough to remind me how she had been trying to make the point for some time. She was right, I was wrong.

Thanks to a lesson taught to me by my son, I decided that my job from then on was to shut up and have fun out there, which I always did but seldom displayed. I now needed to do more than to try to keep my anger in check. My goal was to show Andy, not through my words but as an example, how to enjoy himself. No matter what happened the next day at the ballpark, I promised myself, things were going to change around the dugout as far as I was concerned.

To my surprise, it wasn't as hard as I'd thought.

What also changed about how I saw myself and my temperament was a family holiday gathering when all five of us O'Neill boys were gathered in Dad's kitchen, wondering when the griddle cakes would be coming. As Dad searched feverishly for the pancake mix, Pat, a baseball guru, asked my father the dreaded question.

"Dad, which one of us was the worst sport?" Pat asked.

Oh, no, I thought as I waited for the answer. Not only did we have to compete throughout childhood, now we had to compete about the competition! My brain went back to Mike and Pat competing in Little League, back when I was underneath the bleachers in the gravel area playing around and getting Bub's Daddy grape gum stuck in my curls. Other memories turned to Kevin during hockey games. None of us won any awards when it came to handling defeat well. I hated losing. Robert suffered horribly through losses. He wiped tears off his glove at age twelve and argued with umpires like a pro in his early teens.

Dad's judgment had to be between the two of us. Robert and I leaned against each other and against the familiar Formica counter in the kitchen, looking out at the backyard where home-run derbies had ruined many family dinners by ending with a brouhaha.

Not taking long to give his answer, Dad, without batting an eyelash at my other brothers, walked closer and closer to Robert and me. His hair was uncombed, his pants seemingly held up by his slippers, and he raised his left arm—the same arm that threw terrifying curveballs—and targeted . . . my brother! Aha—I *wasn't* the biggest crybaby in the family.

I was off the hook.

If the 1996 Yankees season had been something of a fairy tale come true, 1998 was even more magical.

No Hollywood screenwriter could have written a better script for all the drama, suspense, and glory it held for us. For me there was to be great vindication in getting to take on some of the rivals who had beaten us in years past—including both the Seattle Mariners, who'd kept us from the championship in 1995, as well as the Cleveland Indians, who'd rained on our 1997 parade.

How much I was looking forward to having the last word, I can't say, although this may have been the year that George Steinbrenner dubbed me his "ultimate warrior." It was humbling and embarrassing enough to be praised that way by George, but Michael Kay never let me hear the end of it. Before every interview, I had to warn him emphatically not to bring it up.

Nonetheless, I was certainly ready to go when the Mariners arrived at Yankee Stadium for an important game, and I got a crucial hit off Bobby Ayala to put our team in a position to win the game. Afterward I just screamed toward their dugout. Payback feels darn good when you're on the delivering side. They had my number for a while, but not in that game.

In this historic year, in which we won an astonishing 114 games during the regular season, such victories were the dominant theme, except for one 4–3 loss to the Detroit Tigers in the seventeenth inning on July 20. That was the first game of a doubleheader yet! How do you play seventeen innings and lose and then go out and play again?

It was the type of day that challenges a major-leaguer at his core, that puts the battle into perspective—because no matter how good a team you are, and no matter how many wins you have, you always want to win one more game.

Joe Torre suggested I take off the next day to rest, but I told him that I was fine to come back out and play. Disappointed about the Detroit game though I was, no way was I going to miss a moment of what we were experiencing—the season of a lifetime, making history with every game.

Over in the National League, 1998 was history-making time, too, for the St. Louis Cardinals' Mark McGwire and the Chicago Cubs' Sammy Sosa as the two slugged it out, chasing Roger Maris's 61-home-run record—not unlike the Mickey Mantle–Maris chase of Babe Ruth's record in 1961.

As much as the public was following the contest, I and many of my major-league peers were watching just as closely. McGwire's and Sosa's athletic prowess and their mutual respect during their contest represented all major-leaguers in the most honorable, exemplary way. Many of us, yours truly included, had hit a lot of home runs, but not 60 of them in any one season!

Sammy was slamming home runs at a torrid pace, and so was Mark.

Both were destined to pass Maris's record, and they were both slated to do it in the old 154-game stretch.

Their thundering drumroll was heard, as it happened, when the Yankees were playing the Red Sox in Boston and I was in the on-deck circle. All of a sudden, there was a roar from the crowd, and I looked up to the Diamond Vision—the ballpark's massive electronic screen—and read the news: Mark McGwire had hit his 60th home run.

In the cool, damp Boston air, a feeling of enchantment came over the night as we all watched the replay. In those moments the historical significance of Mark's hitting 60 home runs, one away from Maris (that he and Sammy would later surpass with 70 and 63 home runs, respectively, for the season) made our world suddenly smaller. Here we were playing our archrival Red Sox, and in another ballpark Mark McGwire had just tied Ruth. For a brief moment, baseball history was connected by only six degrees of separation.

Every time I played at Fenway Park during that season and Dad wasn't there, I wondered if his vow to make a road trip hadn't been overly optimistic. But at the end of 1998's season, he scheduled the trip to come up on September 9 with my brother Robert—what would turn out to be Chick's last road trip to see me play.

Dad *had* to make that last pilgrimage to Fenway to be with me. There was no more pretending that nothing was wrong with his health. He was by now noticeably out of breath when moving around, and even the effort it required for him to talk on the phone made his regular breathing more pronounced.

Argue though we might that a trip might be too exhausting for him, his will to see that game was so intense that he wouldn't let it bother him.

Dad didn't want to be treated as diminished in any way and, being of the mind-set that we all carry our own load, didn't feel he needed help.

Not that we wanted him to feel that way, but the truth of the matter was that he *did* need help in getting around. Walking for an extended period of time tired him out drastically.

When I heard the story of the mountains he moved to get there, even I, Chick O'Neill's son, couldn't believe the level of determination he had shown.

For starters, the cabdriver dropped him and Robert a half mile away from Fenway Park, because he didn't want to get stuck in traffic, even though Robert told him to get closer. They walked the rest of the way.

To add insult to injury, when they arrived at the ballpark, Dad leaning on Robert's arm, the ticket-booth attendant informed them both that the will-call ticket window had no tickets for them.

"Why don't we just go back to the hotel and watch the game on television?" Robert pleaded with our father after surveying both Dad's health and the enormous walk ahead of them just to get into the stadium, not to mention the need to weave through the dense crowds.

No way, Dad insisted. He had come too far to quit. He wanted one more trip around the block. Fenway, as charming as it is, is tough for anyone with a disability.

Dad's will to see me play that day at Fenway was so strong that when I turned around and looked into the stands, there he was sitting beside George Steinbrenner, after Robert proved to the ticket-booth personnel that they were part of my family.

My father's being in the stands mattered more to me than words could express. Fenway Park could have been filled to capacity with standing-room-only crowds, but I knew where my father was sitting. I could feel his presence, like a bright beam of sunlight shining on me when I took to right field.

After Dad arrived, I went on to hit two home runs—one of them to center field, and in Fenway Park that's a good ways away from home plate. In this game I was definitely swinging for the fences for my father.

There was great poignancy to our celebration afterward, at least for me. Dad was just his jovial self, kidding me about how George Steinbrenner had told Robert that he wished he had twenty-five guys like me.

Dad was so proud. What could I say? I only shook my head, laughing out of embarrassment.

Inside, another emotion was brewing, one I had no way to fathom, having never been down this road before. Nobody had to tell me that my father was mortal, but the cold, hard fact that his traveling days were over and that we would no longer share what we had shared—because of infirmity, old age, or by death—still dealt an awful blow to my heart.

Robert and I had little time to discuss our father's state. "Dad's not getting around very well," my brother confided in me during a brief exchange we had in the Boston hotel room. I nodded, acknowledging without words the worry we were both feeling.

Family Days at Yankee Stadium suddenly came to mind, and I remembered those moments when Dad had been on the field with me, soaking in all the history. The thought that we would never have another one of those days was too much to bear.

For obvious reasons, Dad and Robert didn't continue with the team up to Toronto, though I would have liked it if that had been possible. My father had really enjoyed the SkyDome in previous visits.

But in spite of his physical absence at the game, Dad's magical energy that spurred me at Fenway must have stuck around, because I had another two-homer game against the Blue Jays that very next day. Hitting two home runs in back-to-back games was something I had never done before in my career.

For the rest of this monumental year, I felt all the good-luck-charm glimmers of my father's sending me his proud thoughts from home as he followed the goings-on by satellite.

I felt Dad's glow and got to give him the news that when the 1998 regular season came to a close, Bernie Williams and I had become the first pair of Yankee outfielders in sixty-five years to bat .300 or better in four consecutive seasons. That hadn't been done since Babe Ruth and Earle Combs (who both batted .300 or higher in the four consecutive seasons of 1927 to 1933).

The last day of the season belonged to Bernie Williams, who, having won the 1998 batting title, came out of the locker room in his sweats to take a curtain call for the fans. The crowd's thundering fanfare could not have been more deserved or more graciously received than by my fellow Yankee and great friend.

The season's closing game was memorable to me for other reasons, as it happened to be Joe DiMaggio Day at Yankee Stadium. At the pregame festivities, Paul Simon was on hand to perform "Mrs. Robinson"— a song that had further immortalized "Joltin' Joe," and DiMaggio loved every minute of it, listening to fifty-five thousand people singing along in homage.

I was thrilled to be able to meet Mr. DiMaggio one last time. Just being in the same dugout as him gave me goose bumps.

All the players felt the same way about having him back in the Bronx. DiMaggio, Yogi Berra, Phil Rizzuto—these guys *were* the New York Yankees. We were just renting locker-room space. These guys were living legends, icons kids dreamed of becoming, and we were tickled to stand anywhere near them. Whenever these guys walked into that Yankee dugout, the stadium took on one voice—that of reverence.

Some years earlier, at Old Timers' Day at Yankee Stadium, I had asked Mr. DiMaggio to sign a baseball bat—which he had declined because, as someone told me later, he rarely signed autographs and the like. Understanding, I never asked him again.

I was asking for the bat to be signed not really for me, but for the collection of signed baseball bats I'd started for my kids when they began getting excited about memorabilia—a collection that eventually would include almost thirty signed bats of their favorite players. I came to every city prepared with "the list" Andy and Aaron had given me, telling me whose signature to get on a bat. Naturally, they wanted the All-Stars. All of them. Wanting to be a good dad, I did my best and eventually collected some very impressive names. The lineup included Barry Bonds, Mark McGwire, Sammy Sosa, Ken Griffey Jr., Manny Ramirez, Mike Piazza, and the rest of my kids' personal all-star team.

It had been almost six years since DiMaggio had declined to sign the bat, and so when Joe DiMaggio—on Joe DiMaggio Day—approached me in the locker room, asking, "You still want that bat signed?" for a split second I was too floored to answer.

Then I caught myself, quickly saying, "Yes, sir!" and I raced off to get that bat. Flying out of the locker room at full gallop to the bat rack in the dugout, I felt all of seven years old. I grabbed one of my bats and flew right back into the clubhouse.

Joe DiMaggio signed it for me, smiled, and wished me luck.

What was the reason he waited those years to sign it? Was it just a change of mood? The particular circumstances of the different occasions? Or was it because I'd passed his test for being a true Yankee? Whatever had motivated him, it meant all the more when, less than a year later, DiMaggio passed away on March 8, 1999.

His gift of signing that bat was a treasure to me and to my kids. It stands out in the collection because his signature is quite legible. Many of the older ballplayers had beautiful signatures—unlike many players today—and Joe DiMaggio had a truly elegant, fluid script signature that looks more like an artist's signature, not an athlete's.

Little time was left to revel in our record-breaking season, not with the playoffs upon us. The Texas Rangers had a great team, and we knew they'd be looking to go to the World Series via beating New York in the ALCS. Seattle had the same hopes, as usual, and the team was making some noise in the playoffs. Edgar Martinez—who has one of the sweetest swings in the game of baseball—was fueling the Mariners' offense. I have always marveled at Edgar's hitting. He is as good as it gets from the right side.

The playoffs were as nuts as we'd expected, the media coverage cranking up several notches, fans everywhere rooting us on—including our very own Billy Crystal. One of the biggest Yankee fans you could ever meet, Billy used to love to come out during batting practice and get in the cage and shag fly balls in the outfield. He was good at it, too, and I could tell that he had a lot of natural ability. Billy was out there for every playoff game, cheering at the top of his lungs.

Our confidence was buoyed to an all-time high. If we got behind in a game, our secret weapon was knowing we had Darryl Strawberry in our arsenal to hit a pinch-hit grand slam to win it for us—because things like that kept happening. Somebody always managed to be the hero on any given night.

We always knew we'd win the game; it was just a matter of who would step up to do the job. Losing was not an option. The hardest part about the whole playoff picture was the fact that, because we clinched so early that year, we hadn't played a game that really meant anything in months.

We also knew that if any of the teams now looking strong—the Red Sox, the Indians, the Braves, and the Rangers—snuck up on us, the importance of our 114 wins would be erased if we fell at all short of going all the way. If we were truly a team for the ages, we had a mandate to win the World Series.

With everyone gunning for us, the playoffs turned out to be more frightening than the World Series. In the five-game division series, anything can happen and usually does. Nonetheless, we sailed past the Texas Rangers and began the seven-game American League Championship Series against Cleveland—a team I was eager to defeat.

But the Indians were tough. We won the first game, they won the second and the third and, lo and behold, we came back to win in Game Four, never looking back. After winning the fifth and sixth games, we had won the ALCS 4–2.

We were going back to the World Series!

The San Diego Padres—having won the NLCS against Atlanta—looked ready to take us on. They had Trevor Hoffman, while we had Mariano Rivera—who had achieved legendary status as a closer in 1998. This was definitely *his* year. It got to the point where just to see him warming up in the bullpen became a huge mental factor in the game that bothered the opposition. Between Trevor and Mo, it was sure to be a battle of the closers.

From the Padres' standpoint, this had to be Tony Gwynn's World Series as well, as he was the greatest pure hitter in the game. He hit a home run over my head, and—as a hitter and as a person—they don't come much better and nicer than Tony Gwynn.

Gwynn is the prototypical Hall of Fame hitter. Whenever he came up to the plate, no matter how much extra effort a pitcher employed to get him out, he tenaciously battled back, working the count full until he either drew a walk or got a hit. Gwynn was most dangerous when the pitcher thought he might win the battle, like when he was 0–2 in the count. He always managed to get that timely hit for his team.

The Padres had other ammunition, no doubt. But we had the lineup of a lifetime and the Yankee Passion—the thousands of fans who decided to fly cross-country bringing it with them all the way to San Diego. This was a phenomenon I'd seen before, but I never ceased to be amazed by the depths to which our fans went to root for us.

There were Yankee fans *everywhere*. They met us at the airport. They cheered us on in the hotel elevators and lobby. They waited outside the ballpark for us, and whenever I stepped out of the visiting dugout in San Diego, there they were in the stands, en masse, yelling and screaming for us. We might have been wearing our road gray jerseys, but it felt like we were at home because of the concentration of Yankee fans from New York right by the third-base dugout.

During the Series I made an error and thought I'd really messed things up, but Scott Brosius saved me when he went deep to dead center late in the game off Trevor Hoffman. I wanted to hug Brosius at home plate I was so happy.

During this Series I had moments to catch my breath long enough to look around with admiration at my teammates.

There were many hurrah stories within the larger story of the regular season and postseason. Jorge Posada had emerged as a fine young catcher, shepherded in by none other than Joe Girardi, who had a true leader mentality. Rare is the person who will train someone else to take his job, as Joe did with Jorge Posada, teaching him the art of game-calling—so vital for a catcher, who is basically the only player on the field who actually sees the full picture. Joe also showed Jorge how to work with the young pitching staff and with the veterans. For that reason and many others, Joe is one of the few people I would recommend kids' copying as a role model. I would trust Joe Girardi with anything and everything that I have in life.

Derek Jeter had come to the league at the perfect time in 1996, and by this World Series, his future Hall of Fame status was on the big screen for all to see. Derek had the best instincts of anyone and played the game with perfection.

There were the perfectly timed trades. There were the free-agent signings. There was the big rookie surprise in Shane Spencer. Shane had an earth-shattering month, smacking ten home runs to end the season in a blaze of glory. In the first playoff action of his career, in Texas, Spencer had hit some big home runs, helping us to defeat the Rangers in our search for the championship.

Scott Brosius had a career year and was the comic relief we needed in the clubhouse. And, as we came into Game Four of the World Series, having swept the Padres so far, Brosius was what we needed to start the final play to end the World Series.

And suddenly it was all over.

"Hit on the ground on a hop to Brosius, fields, throws across to first. Ball game over! World Series over! Yankees win! *Thhheeee* Yankees win!" John Sterling announced.

"The Yankees are World Champions in a dream season—125 wins—unheard of. In our life we will probably never see this again," Michael Kay added.

Nobody could have said it better than those two guys. They put into precise perspective what we as players had felt all season long.

What we accomplished in 1998 impressed me more a few years after it all unfolded. I was then able to sit back and see how the pieces of the puzzle had fit together—how Joe Torre, Don Zimmer, and Mel Stottlemyre (who was our pitching coach and as respected in that dugout as anyone) had done it. They were the perfect combination at the helm of this juggernaut.

This is probably why the Yankees have been such a fabled team, from the famous Babe Ruth "called shot" to our 1998 championship team: The franchise managed to win when it counted.

Not only did we have talent this year, but everybody had career years. Everything clicked beyond belief, certainly exceeding Yankees general manager Brian Cashman's expectations by epic proportions.

Having been a member of this team, I feel that this was the *greatest* team I've ever played on, and I believe we deserve to be ranked among the top teams of all time.

Besides, 1998 was all the more important a year to me because it was the last full baseball season, from start to finish, that Dad was able to experience.

——— • ———

TEN

The Toughest Season

Words I'd never spoken out loud stuck in my throat during the car ride from the hospital in Columbus en route to the airport to leave for the 1999 season's spring training. Finally I turned to Nevalee and put my question into words. "Is this the last time I'm going to see Dad?" I asked her.

Neither one of us knew the answer, although we were praying with all our hearts that this was only a rough patch and that he would rally. I clung to that hope, needing to keep the faith as he'd taught me to do.

But it was tough to stay positive once I arrived at spring training, something he'd rarely missed. Not many years earlier, Dad was there in the stands, watching two to three games a day, and now he was in a hospital bed in Ohio. Coronary artery disease doesn't discriminate between people or between baseball seasons.

Legends Field that first week in Tampa in February looked the same as usual. The ballpark was the same, the fences were the same, the grass was as thick and green as ever, and the same bright-eyed, excited kids filled the stands. But Dad's absence this year was painfully noticeable.

Some days I found an escape from my worries about him by just focusing on my game. Most days my efforts not to let his health battles affect my average at the plate were not successful. For anyone in my position—losing the person you love, the one who has been your constant guiding light—it's hard to separate by trying to construct boundaries.

How could I say to myself that during batting practice I wasn't going to think about the fact that my father might be dying? I was human. Not a robot. I bleed. I cry. I punch watercoolers. I cry some more. I worry. I'm a person.

By March my conversations with him caused me so much worry that there were many nights—not knowing if one of them might be his last—that it killed me I couldn't be at his bedside. But, for his sake, I had to be optimistic. I had to be for him what he'd been for me, the ultimate optimist. I had to take Dad's place and be the one with the rah-rah attitude that he would battle back and win this fight.

"You're *going* to be fine!" I said to him on phone call after phone call, filling my voice with the same confidence he'd exuded all those years when he'd tell me, "You hit that ball right on the button!"

Most of the family was back in Ohio, while I was hundreds of miles away in Florida feeling rather helpless. Yet, to my incredible relief, Dad in fact rallied and ended up having a steady spring.

There was a duality to life for me. As a baseball player, I was in good form—playing and hitting well, feeling fit physically. On the inside I was hurting. Whatever the prognosis was for my father, he was no longer his old vital, energetic self, and it upset me deeply.

And then, in March, came more upsetting news when Joe Torre shocked us with the announcement that he had prostate cancer. Suddenly a somber mood descended upon everyone at spring training.

Now it was not only my own father I was praying for, but also a father figure of mine and many of my fellow Yankees.

We all had Joe in our thoughts and prayers on March 18 when he underwent surgery at Barnes-Jewish Hospital in St. Louis. If anyone could get through this—no one in the Yankee extended family would disagree—it was Joe Torre. Joe was tough, as all catchers must be, having to endure perhaps the most pummeling and pain of anyone on the field, just as they must be smart and in charge enough to be winning game-callers. Joe was in charge, all the time. And he was a catcher at heart, always.

After a successful surgery, Joe took the time off that he needed, recuperated, and was back in full swing by the summer's start. All was well. Thank God, Joe had prevailed, showing us how you beat cancer.

Meanwhile, our season was off and running with the hoisting of the 1998 championship flag in the Bronx on Opening Day.

For me there were some personal victories that came early, particularly in the case of facing my pitching nemesis, Jesse Orosco. Jesse was one of the toughest pitchers I ever batted against, and he just plain wore me out. Each at-bat was a saga. His toughness stemmed from the fact that he had a unique delivery that fooled hitters. But on April 14 of this year, in a game against Baltimore, I finally got the better of Orosco when, during my last at-bat against him, I hit a home run and then, as fate would have it, never had to face him again. I also recorded my 1,000th career RBI in that game.

Another pitcher I used to dread facing, who had come on board with the Yankees this season, was none other than Roger Clemens—with his fistful of Cy Young Awards. As much as I hated to face him as a pitcher, I loved having him on my side twice as much.

When he first arrived at spring training, I wondered how Clemens would feel about the fact that he had always worn the number 21—throughout his career with the Sox and the Jays—just as I had always worn number 21. In the Bronx, Yankee fans seemed to know me as someone with a number tacked onto his last name—O'Neill #21.

Roger never made an issue of it, never once asking me to relinquish the number. I kept mine, he took a new number, and Roger Clemens was in Cy Young form for the start of the 1999 season. I would never forget his graciousness and respect in this act of friendship to me, as well as his professionalism as a ballplayer and teammate. "The Rocket" was truly a team player, wanting to be one of us, compete alongside us, befriend us, and celebrate with us—we hoped!—come October.

Had there been an issue over who would get to wear number 21, it might have become a problem with an intense group of loyal fans that populated the stands above right field. Having my own cheering section out there—fans I affectionately called the "Right-Field Faithful"—was such a phenomenon for me. It made the victories that much sweeter and helped to take the edge off the disappointments and ease some of the harder days I was having with Dad's health being so up and down.

My father had told me early on that it was important how fans perceived me, that my career success and happiness would be linked to their approval. As long as I showed the fans that I cared about them and about the game of baseball, my father believed, they would be there for me through the highs and the lows.

The Right-Field Faithful were amazing! Never in my travels had I seen a group of fans that cared so much about their right fielder. These fans held up signs for me, cheered for me like nuts, and serenaded me on a daily basis with tons of encouragement.

But I was mystified. Why was there such a group of die-hard Yankee fans? Why *was* there a Right-Field Faithful? Why did these folks like me? What did they see in me that made them so devoted?

The answer that made sense had to do with the extraordinary feeling of love in the air toward this team. It was the Yankee Passion, it was the New York melting pot, it was the family that made up our team—a bunch of great human beings, managed with true inspiration by Joe Torre, Don Zimmer, and Mel Stottlemyre. You couldn't write a better book on how to win than just by going over the modus operandi of these three men and seeing the way they steered this team.

Yankee fans continued to show me that they are the greatest fans anywhere. They root with their hearts. On the streets of New York City, they would walk up to me, roll up a shirtsleeve, and reveal a tattoo of the Yankees logo.

They had nicknames for me too numerous and too embarrassing to recall. They remembered stats about me that I couldn't even remember. They knew that *Grease* was my favorite movie, and they knew my favorite songs—which became my theme songs that were played at Yankee Stadium, always in the same order.

My first at-bat was always to John Mellencamp's "Crumblin' Down." I loved the drum solo in that song! The second at-bat was to Bon Jovi's "Keep the Faith." My third at-bat was Norman Greenbaum's "Spirit in the Sky." My fourth at-bat—and we usually all got four at-bats—was to Bruce Springsteen's "Tenth Avenue Freeze-Out"—by which point the fans were rockin' down the house.

If I had a fifth at-bat, the song was always "Baba O'Reilly" by the Who. The Who got shut out some nights—on a bad night or when I didn't get enough at-bats—but when we were on a hot streak, their song was blasting in the Bronx.

Fans noticed that, while other players changed songs and the order of songs, I didn't. They'd say that they missed hearing my fifth song because I didn't get up to the plate five times.

To have such fans is perhaps something that no player experiences until he puts on the pinstripes. And it wasn't only fans in New York who got behind us; we had fans across the nation cheering us on in every city we visited. In my opinion it wasn't merely because of the talent of the players. Rather, it was because of the character of our players. This is something my father taught me, what I learned in my own experiences, and what I believe: Character does matter to fans. They want to root for good human beings.

The Yankees were all about character. The way we won was phenomenal, but the side stories were equally important, and the side stories made us perceived as a caring group of people and as individuals who had our own share of adversity and had overcome against the odds.

Dad used to tell me that you can't please everyone all the time, and you'll go nuts if you try. "Paul," he'd say, intoning it in a way that made it sound as if no one but him had ever said this, "just be true to yourself."

Those were simple but wise words that often fell upon my deaf and stubborn ears. But over time I'd learned to accept criticism—even where unfounded—and to deal with controversy when it reared its head. I learned that by being true to myself, though I would not be loved by every person all the time, I would still be loved by the ones that mattered most—the fans!

The Right-Field Faithful in the Bronx meant the *entire* world to me! They treated me like one of the family.

Standing in right field and watching them hold up their signs of affection often sent me back to Dad's prediction that what I thought was the worst day in my life—after hearing news that I was traded to the Yankees—would become the best thing that ever happened. How had he known? Could he ever have seen that I would be here with all these World Series rings, playing for the greatest franchise in sports history? I could never have had the love in Cincinnati that I had in New York from those right-field fans. It wouldn't have existed anywhere else in baseball.

Somehow the Right-Field Faithful picked up on Dad's theme of hitting right on the button and created a fan logo for me that showed a bull's-eye target in the center of the *O* of their O'NEILL #21 signs. It still boggles my mind to think that anyone would take the time to make a sign at home, bring it to the ballpark, and display it for me. I never thought I was so important that I deserved a sign, a baseball card, or any type of recognition so public in nature. Whether it was deserved or not, I genuinely love them for going to the trouble of making the signs and holding up those bull's-eyes as a reminder of their support.

After Dad's health had been stable for much of the spring, in June he suffered a heart attack, making that one of the worst months of my life. His condition was getting worse by the day. A ray of hope lay in the possibility of an experimental procedure that had been showing promise. As we investigated that possibility, my only other hope was that he'd somehow find a way, with help from the heavens, to beat this disease. If any human being could, it was Chick O'Neill. I had to believe that. After all, miracles happen every day.

In baseball history a miraculous occurrence took place July 18, on what had been declared Yogi Berra Day. Following the loss of Joe DiMaggio—a monument to him had been unveiled earlier in the season at the stadium—the fans needed to see some of the glory days relived. After Yogi was fired as manager of the Yankees, he refused to visit Yankee Stadium for years. But thankfully, as it so happened, George Steinbrenner had made up with Yogi in grand style, and all was once again well in the Bronx.

Yogi is such a wonderful person and a beloved Yankee that having him in the ballpark—on his own official day—allowed all of us to shake hands with history. You can't mention the Yankees without mentioning names like Babe Ruth, Lou Gehrig, Joe DiMaggio, Mickey Mantle, Roger Maris, Whitey Ford, Phil Rizzuto, and, of course, the inimitable Yogi Berra.

The sunny summer-afternoon game between the Yankees and the Expos started off in perfect fashion, as Don Larsen threw out the first pitch to Yogi. What could be better than seeing two legends take the field? Yogi was back in the Bronx, alongside the man who had hooked up with him in 1956 for one of the most famous World Series games of all times, the Perfect Game.

Although everybody in the park was thrilled to see Yogi again, nobody expected that another Dynamic Duo would be tossing some magic back and forth. Maybe David Cone and Joe Girardi were given some heavenly inspiration from Yogi and Larsen.

In any event, something very magical was happening, and we had no idea until it became apparent in the eighth inning that Cone and Girardi had been playing a perfect game of catch. Montreal had not gotten one hit off us the entire afternoon—so far. I had made a diving catch early on in the game to contribute to the cause.

The ninth inning was tense, just at it had been a year earlier when Boomer Wells was going for a perfect game. We were all rooting for David Cone—a really great guy in the clubhouse and a friend to all of us during his playing tenure with the Yankees—and so we were all pressing for him to come through. Neither Bernie nor I wanted any sinking liners hit to us in the outfield. The ninth inning is when perfect games are suddenly lost and no-hitters are broken up—even shutouts ruined.

This is the precise inning when the opposing team has taken it into their heads that they will not be no-hit or shut out. No one player wants to be the last out in a history-making perfect game.

All of a sudden there was a pop-up, a majestic pop-up that seemed to hang up there endlessly. Scott Brosius came in from third, caught the ball as it plummeted to earth, and the game was over!

Cone had done it! Yogi and Larsen couldn't believe what they had witnessed. They were as ecstatic as the young screaming fans. Nobody could believe what had happened that afternoon in the Bronx.

I couldn't even believe it—two friends of mine, David Wells and David Cone, had pitched two of the only fifteen perfect games in regular-season history and had been the only Yankees to accomplish this feat—and in back-to-back years. If I hadn't played in the game, I would have thought it was all a dream.

They say that lightning doesn't strike twice. In my life I had now been struck by the lightning of three perfect games—Tom Browning's, David Wells's, and David Cone's.

After the game Nevalee and I headed off to a huge Bruce Springsteen concert, along with friends Tim and Jane O'Neill (no relation to me), who were in town visiting and had been guests of mine at the game.

In the car I marveled at our good fortune—a perfect game, a concert by the Boss, family and friends, all in one day. Only in New York!

Pressure was building as the end of the regular season approached. To earn our status as a dynasty, we had to have our back-to-back

World Series wins, and we knew that the playoffs would be fierce. The high expectations were even starting to rattle our nerves. Then, on September 14, in a crucial moment against the Blue Jays at the SkyDome in Toronto, I hit a grand slam that propelled us to a big team win. From that point on, we were rolling as a team in our play-off quest.

As for the status of Dad's health, there was a bit of encouragement. His physician in Columbus had recommended he undergo the experimental procedure being done at Lenox Hill Hospital in New York City that had the potential to allow him to function normally again. Hoping only for the best, I also felt reassured that he would be closer and I could see him more often.

In the midst of what was going on off the field, on October 2, I was injured playing against the Tampa Devil Rays at Tropicana Field. There was a foul ball that was popped up in my direction, and I just went after it and after it, and I smacked directly into the right-field wall, coming away with a cracked rib. The wall didn't give an inch, so I guess it won that battle.

My approach was to try to play hard through that injury, as I did with all injuries. But it was tough to do, and the team physician ordered me to rest. For my entire professional career, I had always opted to play hard through injury for a few reasons. One was the way I was raised. With our parents' work ethic, if one of us was only mildly sick, we went to school. Colds didn't keep us down. We were expected to get up and go to school without saying a word.

Another reason was my own resistance to being out of the game. Part of being a player is being able to stay healthy, and though some players may have wanted the time off, I looked at the DL as the *dreaded* list.

I figured that once I was put on the disabled list, it would play itself into one big nightmare. No sooner would I have gotten within reach of my goals for the season than to have them ended by the DL. And when I came off it, the first game would be one big smack in the face, and I'd have to start from scratch. This was the way I perceived even taking a day off for some healthy rest. Why sit down?

Some players on our team have dealt with the DL well, but a "cheer-leader" on the bench was not what I wanted to be, and some of the best games I ever had happened on days when other guys might not have played. After all, sitting down would give away at-bats that could be crucial to my year!

I also never liked the disabled list because it gets a player out of rhythm. However, playing through pain can get a player out of rhythm, too, as I found out during this year. Playing through pain is more frus-trating emotionally than physically. In baseball there really is no time to recover. There aren't any weekends or series of days off in a row to rest whatever part of your body hurts.

Many of my teammates felt as I did, and we all had fun talking to trainer Gene Monahan about our injuries and then whispering to him, "Don't tell Joe," as he walked out of the trainer's room. Joe, however, was the best at letting players rest through an injury without making them feel guilty.

Joe was extremely sensitive to what I was going through this year, as were my coaches and teammates. In every spare minute during the playoffs, I was racing down to see Dad at Lenox Hill. There was still hope that the procedure would be successful, but it was probably apparent that worrying about my father had taken its toll on me, physi-cally and emotionally. For the remainder of the time, the playoffs did offer some bright spots.

It was a joy having the Rocket—who is a Texan—on the mound for us when we were in the division playoffs in Texas and seeing how much he really wanted to win a game as a Yankee. In the first inning of Game

Three, New York favorite Darryl Strawberry came up to the plate and hit a dramatic three-run home run, sending our fans who had traveled to Texas with us into the stratosphere. They cheered so loud I could hear them in the locker room, where I was nursing my rib from my Tampa injury. Clemens went on to pitch a shutout for his first seven innings, giving us a 3–0 victory over the Rangers, whom we swept in the division playoffs.

"You ought to have that thing checked," joked the doctors at Lenox Hill Hospital every time I popped in to sit by Dad's side in intensive care. Their levity did make me feel better.

Dad was coherent, constantly thinking of me and wanting me to go home and get some rest. I thought back to his nights running a snow-plow for twenty-four hours, sacrificing everything for us, collapsing from sheer exhaustion. That's what I felt it was necessary for me to do, to face the storm with him and see it through to calmer days. I was keeping the faith.

The American League Championship Series against Boston started off on a terrific note, and what made life better was that the first two games were played at home.

Bernie Williams hit a crucial home run in Game One against our rivals, and that proved to be just what we needed. We won Game Two as well and were up 2–0 when we arrived at Fenway Park for Game Three.

Game Three at Fenway was a tough one for us. Pedro Martinez was masterful on the mound for Boston. He struck me out early, and I knew we were in for a long game. Not pretty, it was an arduous battle, and the Red Sox killed us 13–1. Darryl Strawberry's playoff performances continued to be exciting when he hit another big home run for us in Game Four, locking up a save opportunity for Mariano Rivera.

Since 1996, when he came in as a setup man for John Wetteland, Mo had helped change the game of baseball. In fact, "Lights Out" Rivera was the major reason we won so many World Series championships. People forget that before Mariano you had great starters and you had your great closers. When we made Mariano the setup man for Wetteland, everything changed. Mariano gave us three solid innings, which allowed Joe to have John take over the ninth inning and close out the game with ease. All of a sudden people around the league started paying attention to us and our secret for success, which made for a shift in thinking among managers—that it was no longer enough to have a great starting rotation and a great closer. By making the position of setup man so important, Lights Out helped pave the way for Jeff Nelson and Mike Stanton and other notable setup men around the league to get some well-deserved recognition.

In Game Five, Orlando Hernandez was our man on the mound. "El Duque" was passion personified—locked in with every pitch—and had an incredible personal story of coming all the way to America from Cuba on a little boat, risking his life for the freedom we enjoy in our great nation. El Duque pitched his heart out and won the fifth game for us, with Ramiro Mendoza on the mound for the final out.

As much as the Yankees cheered one another's best moments on the field, there was also tremendous empathy for one another when things weren't going well. Chuck Knoblauch had been a huge help to our team but had been going through some fielding problems. It really pained me, especially when a play didn't go his way, and he disputed the umpire's call, pointing to the ball at first base while the base runner continued to advance. Everyone—fans, players, reporters—was all over him the next day. George Steinbrenner, however, had a different approach. On the plane ride home, he sat next to Chuck and went over the play, clearing the air and consoling Knobby. This was the side of Steinbrenner that few get to see firsthand.

Chuck opted to take himself out of a game and to go home. For a competitive person like him, that was amazing. Beside himself with disappointment, he made the choice to do what was best for the team because, bottom line, he loved New York. After he arrived, he never wanted to play for anyone else and felt lucky to wear the pinstripes— delivering some big hits for us right when we needed them. The night he went home, I felt as bad as I'd ever felt for another player in my entire career.

Of course, we came back to win that series—a huge load off Chuck's mind. He had been such an integral part of our winning the 1998 World Series, and now, for whatever reasons, he found himself in a stretch in which he was just struggling. Yet he was to be invaluable again in the World Series ahead—where we were headed for a second straight year.

The question remained: What team would we face? Over in the National League, the playoff race had been a tight one.

There had been some murmuring of a Subway Series when the Mets won their division series against the Diamondbacks and went on to face the Braves, who had beaten Houston in a close series.

When Mets' catcher Mike Piazza hit a home run in Game Six, it looked like we might have our wish for an all–New York World Championship duke-out, but the Braves came back in the eleventh inning, winning the NLCS.

Our Subway Series hopes had been dashed, but the Braves were dancing in the streets—wanting nothing more than to beat us and avenge our 1996 World Series win over them.

As I continued to stretch myself as far as I could between doing my job for my team and spending every other moment at the ICU with Dad, my emotions were likewise stretched, as taut and frayed as an old rubber band. The experimental procedure had been a success, and my father, ever convinced that he was on the road to recovery, continued to get enjoyment from my game updates. At the same time, another heart attack a month before and a new staph infection and the resulting complications were clouding his future. What kept me going whenever I left Lenox Hill was the thought that the best way to help Dad was to go out and play with everything I had. For the rest, the doctors would do all they could. Ultimately, I knew he was in God's hands.

Game One of the World Series tapped all the Yankees' heart and soul. The Braves' Tom Glavine was scratched right before the game, so he didn't make his scheduled start, leaving Greg Maddux to start in Glavine's place.

Orlando Hernandez started for us, having come into the Series with a 4–0 postseason record. El Duque struck out Chipper Jones in the first inning—a clear statement to the Braves. Chipper came back with a home run, but that was the only hit Hernandez allowed until the end of the seventh inning. In my at-bat in the seventh, I hit a ground ball to Maddux, which he quickly scooped up, tagging me out as I ran to first base.

Suddenly it was the eighth inning, and we were losing 1–0 to the Braves and down to our final six outs. Scott Brosius kicked off the inning with a single, followed by Darryl Strawberry at the plate pinch-hitting for El Duque and coming through with a timely walk. Now there were runners on first and second with nobody out. Chad Curtis was sent in to first to pinch-run for Straw. Chuck Knoblauch came up and laid down a perfect bunt. The bunt advanced the runners to second and third, plus Knobby made it to first base when the Braves dropped the ball attempting to throw him out at first base. A crucial move on Knobby's part allowed Derek Jeter to come up to the plate with the bases loaded and hit a single to tie the game 1–1.

We had wanted to drive Maddux from the game, and we accomplished that goal when he was removed and John Rocker came on in relief. With two Yankees on base, I went up to the plate and worked the count to 3–1. I knew that whoever was on the mound—it doesn't matter who it is in a situation like this—he had to come in with the pitch and throw a strike. I saw my pitch and got a base hit, scoring two runs. We now had a 3–1 lead.

It was Mo time. Mariano came on and closed out the game. Game One had gone to us in dramatic style, giving both our fans watching at home on television and our traveling team of fans their fill of excitement for the night.

Taking a game from the Braves in Atlanta to start the World Series was pivotal.

Game Two brought the added drama of starting off with the announcement of the All-Century Team roster, which included Roger Clemens taking his rightful place in the group of legends. Watching him stand proudly on the stage in his blue pinstripe suit, in honor of the Yankees, wearing the New York Yankees cap, brought tears to my eyes.

Lou Gehrig, another one of the most heroic Yankees, on and off the field, had beat everyone else in votes cast for the All-Century Team. He had died far too young and too unfairly, yet he'd left a legacy of selflessness in baseball that will never be matched by any player.

For all of us to see so many of the legends of the game standing there on the field was mind-boggling. Not only that, but seeing icons like Sandy Koufax and Willie Mays—in person!—made us feel like such kids again.

Mays rendered me speechless. He was my childhood idol, and he remains my idol today.

What struck me about Sandy was realizing what he had achieved in such a short time—leading the league with the lowest ERA for five straight years, leading in wins in three years, and then having his career cut short when an injury at age thirty-one forced his retirement. That age is typically the prime of a baseball player's career. In my case it was at age thirty-one that I had just begun to hit my stride. What he might have gone on to accomplish is hard to imagine.

In interviews hitters are often asked that if we could step back in time and face a pitcher of any bygone era, what pitcher would it be?

What I used to say to that one was, "Well, I'll tell you, I don't know who I would want to have pitch to me, but I sure am glad I never faced Sandy Koufax!" In fact, meeting him, the first thing I said to Koufax himself was, "Man, am I glad I didn't have to face you!"

He laughed, but I was quite serious.

Sandy Koufax was a pitcher who was unhittable. If you were a left-handed hitter, you were even less likely to get a good pitch to hit. Not in my dreams would I have wanted to face him.

The All-Century Team announcements sprinkled some magic on Game Two for us, and the game started off with Knoblauch and Jeter getting back-to-back hits. I came up to the plate and singled off Kevin Millwood, allowing Knobby to score.

David Cone had a three-run lead by the time he came in to pitch. We won the game 7–2, and we were feeling confident, having taken both games in Atlanta. We flew home—literally and figuratively in the clouds—knowing that the momentum was on our side for the next two games in Yankee Stadium.

But the momentum had swung the other way at Lenox Hill Hospital. To my anguish, instead of improving, Dad was weakening by the hour. Mom was staying at our house by now, and on Tuesday I had driven her to the hospital, remaining there with my father right up until I had to leave for Yankee Stadium.

To see him so weak—the infection complicated by pneumonia, his lungs and kidneys threatening failure—was devastating because it contrasted so starkly with the hugeness of his lifelong presence on this earth. Dad was mostly out of it, but every now and then it seemed that he knew I was there and was trying to communicate to me the message that had been his life's gift to me—not to worry, but to go out there and win tomorrow. He made me believe that he would do the same.

With all that weighing on me, I went to the ballpark for Game Three—pitched by Andy Pettitte—and singled to tie the game in the first inning. Later Joe Girardi made a fantastic throw to third base to get Brett Boone, who was attempting to steal third. Jason Grimsley relieved Pettitte and did a great job, followed by Jeff Nelson, who came on after him and was terrific. We were down 5–1, but Tino hit a home run to get us back in the game. By the eighth inning, we were down only by two runs, 5–3. Joe Girardi got a hit, and Knoblauch hit an amazing home run to tie up the game. In the ninth inning, Mo was called in and took care of business. Girardi threw out Otis Nixon, who was attempting to steal second base.

We went into extra innings with just one advantage—we were the home team and had the chance to end the game. Chad Curtis delivered a home run to win it for us 6–5, to the sound of a thunderous roar from the crowd. How many times does a fan get to see a walk-off home run in a World Series?

We were now up 3–0 in games, and while we had to expect that Atlanta would come at us with all they had for Game Four, the prize was getting closer to our grasp.

When I arrived home late that night, it was hard to get to sleep. My emotions and thoughts were swinging like a pendulum as I tried to visualize a turnaround for Dad, driving myself crazy thinking what I could do or say when I went to see him in the morning. Just as I had managed to calm myself by remembering all the times that Chick O'Neill had known for absolute certain that tomorrow would be a bright day—no matter what the crisis—the phone rang.

It was 2:30 A.M. Before I picked up the phone, I knew what it was. Something told me. There just felt like something devastating in the sound of that jangling ring. This was the call I absolutely couldn't emotionally handle. It was a call from the hospital, informing us that my father had died. The procedure that had promised to save his life would have done so—had it not been for the staph infection he'd caught in the hospital and the complications of pneumonia that ultimately had led to lung and kidney failure.

What I remember for the next five hours is that we all just hugged and cried our eyes out. At some point my mother and Nevalee must have made the phone calls to the rest of my siblings, and maybe they tried to get some rest—I can hardly remember. At six o'clock in the morning, I finally lay down, falling into a turbulent sleep, and I woke up again at nine.

Mom was at the breakfast table, and when I went to sit down next to her, before I even articulated the question, she said to me, "He would want you to play well tonight."

There was nothing more to say. Virginia O'Neill had spoken. Or, rather, Chick O'Neill had spoken through her. Having a death in the family was no excuse for my not going out to play Game Four. It was the World Series, and it was for the team I loved, a team I felt would want me there. The letter that Dad had sent to me so many years ago when I was in the minors said it all: I was *his* son, I was *not* going to miss such an important game. It had to be done.

Not knowing exactly how I was going to get through it, I decided not to tell anyone until after the game—whether we won or lost. Putting on my game face, mentally and spiritually, I went to take a shower, still in a state of shock.

As I emerged from the shower, I overheard Nevalee talking on the telephone, saying to whoever it was, "We've got to get Paul through this."

Dried off and partially dressed, I walked over to Nevalee and quietly asked her, "Who is that?"

She said good-bye, hung up the telephone, looked at me, and answered, "It was Joe Torre."

That was strange. How did he know?

I hadn't told anyone, not a soul. It blew my mind how the Yankees organization found out so quickly about my dad's death. The sensitive way they dealt with me showed me the depth to which the team cared for me, as well as the depth to which George Steinbrenner and Joe Torre cared for me and understood me. Both knew intuitively how I would be feeling this particular day and how badly I wanted to keep my emotions inside.

Joe had been through so much adversity in his own life that I later came to think that, without saying it in so many words, he was here to serve as a guide to show me how to handle this most challenging time of my life.

When I arrived at the ballpark, walking inside was easy for me at first. I walked in—nobody around yet—and went right to my locker. Then the other players started filing inside, and as soon as they saw me, they made a beeline in my direction. The moment the first player came over to me, I lost it.

Luckily, by game time I was able to set my jaw and swallow the terrible lump in my throat.

Game Four of the 1999 World Series was mostly a blur. For a lot of games as far back as Little League, I can remember every pitch and every play, but of Wednesday, October 27, 1999, I can recall almost nothing, except how numb with shock and sadness I felt.

What little I do know is that Roger Clemens pitched a terrific game, with Yankee teamwork providing its best defense and offense, and Mo coming in to close out the game in grand style. As a child in Panama, he had once fashioned a glove out of cardboard, with nothing more than his dreams, his talent, and his will bringing him to this amazing place— Series MVP on behalf of the Yankees in our sweep of Atlanta 4–0, our third championship in just four years.

Throughout that blur of a game, though I didn't look in the direction of the Right-Field Faithful, I felt somehow that many of the fans knew how much I was struggling not to break down and that they were sending me extra support. Whatever it was, I kept it together until right after the last out that signified our victory. Then, as Joe Torre pulled me into the huddle at the pitcher's mound, I couldn't hold back anymore and lost it again as I hugged Joe and Mike Stanton.

Other managers, particularly in the middle of a World Series, would not have allowed me to grieve for my father. Joe Torre was a different type of guy. He was visibly shaken on my behalf, knowing well what Dad meant to me and that no one could replace my father. Joe also knew that I would need a shoulder to lean on now that Dad was gone, and he was going to be that shoulder for me.

Trying not to make a spectacle of myself, I hurried back to the locker room—not allowing myself to take part in the on-field celebration— and found a vacant room, away from the players, fans, and reporters. Dad had been gone less than twenty-four hours, and the reality of it had come to me only now. My impulse, after a lifetime, was to call him first thing after a win and to hear his voice crowing with pride. But I couldn't.

Just then the door opened, and I looked up to see a friendly face, that of Roger Clemens, who'd come in to check on me. Roger gave me a hug, telling me that his thoughts and prayers were with me and my family—which meant so much to me.

Scott Brosius came in right after Roger. During the season Scott had lost his own father, Maury Brosius, to cancer, and he well understood the mourning process I was beginning. Luis Sojo also came to offer his condolences, as he, too, had lost his dad, Ambrosio Sojo, that year. Afterward, my brothers joined me as we shared tears for the father we all had loved so much and now had lost.

When my car approached the church in Powell, Ohio, where Dad's memorial was to be held, my first thought was that he would have approved of the setting, there amid the maples, connected to the land and the changing seasons, as autumn turned to winter.

A lot had happened over the last many days. Though I had wanted to leave immediately for Ohio, Nevalee convinced me to stay for the victory parade, as it was so meaningful to our kids. That meant pushing the memorial back a day later.

After the parade—which was tough—George Steinbrenner came over to me to offer any help he could render, including the use of his plane if I needed it to get home faster. George had a level of vulnerability I had never seen, to the point that his solid demeanor looked shaken on my behalf. The gesture spoke volumes about the true human being he is, and I'll never forget it.

That night I was home in Cincinnati with only a few hours to collect my family, my friends, and my thoughts and head for Columbus for Dad's memorial. Because he was cremated, it would not be a burial, but rather a gathering and a loving send-off.

With so much activity and excitement surrounding the World Series, there'd been little time to prepare emotionally for this day. We woke up, packed the car, and left for Columbus, our dear neighbors joining us for the ride—a ride I will always remember.

It was the final ride to the church in Powell to say good-bye to my father, my childhood hero, my pal, and my mentor. The finality of it opened up the floodgates. My kids had seen me choked up and tearful in the past few days, but they'd never seen me cry this uncontrollably. Thankfully, they seemed to understand—at least on the level that children perceive that something very sad has happened, though not on the level of understanding what a death really means.

Previously and in the months ahead, people whose names I never knew, hundreds of them, would come over to me to say how sorry they were that I'd lost my dad, and then they'd tell me their stories of losing their own loved one. Those tender moments with fans are ones I value even more than the baseball moments, those that capture what life is really about: connection, family, love, community.

No matter what age we are when we lose a parent, no matter how well we understand that the cycle of life will inevitably bring us to this one day, nothing really prepares you for its actuality. Knowing it in advance does little to dull the pain, which to me was a crushing blow.

Gazing at my three kids as we drove toward the church, I thought of how much Papa Chuck had been in gear to teach the next O'Neill generation everything he knew about baseball. When I flashed to that picture of him on the mound in the minors, it occurred to me that he'd looked as good throwing that curveball to my son Andrew when he was in his late sixties as he had back then when he played.

It was my brother Mike who came out to console me and escort us inside after the car arrived at the church. The serenity of the natural outdoor setting was matched by a calming, peaceful feeling inside— thanks to the simplicity of the church's Scandinavian design, the pitched roof and giant wooden beams, the handmade wooden pews, and that pulpit carved from the huge stump of an ancient tree. The way the sun was shining so brightly through the windows created a warm glow that was also fitting for Dad—a good and decent man, a family man, whose spirit was larger than life when he was here with us, larger still now that he was gone.

There were folks who knew my dad because he had coached them as kids. It meant the world to me that they had come and that they'd never forgotten one summer in their young lives when they had Coach O'Neill for Little League. In fact, Dad had coached players besides me who made it to the minor leagues. Scott Holiday was one such player my father really liked. Everyone had a favorite moment or story to tell about Dad. For some the moments occurred on a baseball diamond, and for others they'd taken place during World War II.

Except for one maddening incident—when someone spotted a cameraman in the parking lot taking pictures with a zoom lens—the memorial could not have been more perfect. When I told Robert that I was ready to go after the guy, my brother restrained me.

Then it was time for the eulogies that Molly, Mike, Patrick, and Robert delivered so beautifully. Had I been able to speak, if the finality of their remembrances hadn't torn me up so thoroughly, I would have started as they all had by talking about Dad's Nebraska roots and the fact that he was a paratrooper who had proudly served his country.

No one faulted me for not speaking. They knew that my love for my father was real and that our bond was no exaggeration, something rare and powerful that not all fathers and sons experience. Dad and I lived our bond every single day, and our love for each other was immortal.

His wedding ring was a symbol of the example he had set for me, and Mom gave it to me a year after the memorial. It was thin from decades of wear and tear, representing his undying devotion to my mother and their wonderful marriage and family—and I've worn it ever since she gave it to me, right alongside my own wedding ring.

In the mourning period to come, I would return often to thinking about how intent Dad had been on instilling values in us, and how his faith had provided us such a solid foundation. Because of his efforts, a spiritual strength now resided in me. And in the months ahead, I would turn for solace to the Bible for continuing guidance as to how I should live my life as a person, as a father, as a husband, and even as a ballplayer.

During the memorial, as I allowed myself to grieve freely and fully, a slow shift in my understanding began to take place. I had to let go of the idea that, because he had battled back so many times over the years, he was supposed to have done the same this time. I had to let go of thinking that there was something more that could have been done. It was an eerie feeling, but I needed to accept that when it's over, it's over—there is no more fight left. I wanted to remember him not as he was at the end but as he was throughout the years—strong, indomitable, an outdoor guy sunburned from coaching third base all day to a bunch of Little Leaguers.

If I had spoken at the memorial—or any day later—it would have been simply to say that his love would be with me forever and that his optimism and faith would fill my heart every day of my life.

Since I didn't speak that day, but was granted the privilege of recalling our shared baseball journey together here, as a form of a belated tribute, I return to where I began many pages ago.

It would seem that with Dad no longer alive, our father-son baseball saga was over and that, had we ever been given a chance to retrace our time together, this moment would always mark its end. But the baseball journey wasn't quite over yet, and his presence continued to hover over me in the remarkable days still to come.

———— • ————

ELEVEN

Spirit in the Sky

For me the year started off not as a harbinger of a possible Subway Series, or a three-peat, but rather bittersweet.

There was no way of getting around the fact at Legends Fields that this was the first time I'd put on those cleats, buttoned the pinstripe jersey, pulled down my cap, and dug my fist into my glove without my dad's being at least a phone call away. At the same time, after mourning during the off-season, I was ready to play baseball, ready to enjoy and savor the game I loved. Not a day went by that I didn't think of Dad and miss him, didn't feel a pang of regret for what *he* was missing. But also not a day went by that I didn't feel blessed for the lessons he'd left me.

On Opening Day at Yankee Stadium, I remembered how my father always described it as a clean slate, a chance for every team to start over, throw off disappointments from the past, and create a fresh future to have the season of our lives, both individually and as a team.

In the Bronx there weren't many disappointments from the past when Hall of Famers Phil Rizzuto and Yogi Berra hoisted the championship flag. The place roared and roared. Dad would have loved it, I noted wistfully, just as he would have loved hearing the singing of the national anthem and seeing the Right-Field Faithful packed in the stands with their O'Neill bull's-eye signs.

I wondered what Dad would have thought about all the importance everyone was placing on a possible Subway Series and what he might have said to my concerns. There was always a chance that the Mets wouldn't win the NLCS and make it to the World Series or, worse, that we wouldn't win the ALCS or—the worst-case scenario—that the Yankees could lose to the Mets. Without him there to answer, I reminded myself of the old rule of thumb—that fans always remember the teams who win the World Series, not the teams who lose.

Another subtle and ironic reminder of how life had changed came one day when, after a so-so at-bat, I started to lapse into being mad at myself. Don Zimmer walked over to me, after seeing me mumbling disgustedly and lightly tapping a watercooler.

"I got some bad news, Paul," he began.

I looked up, thinking he was getting ready to warn me that if I wanted to quit, he knew that guy in Columbus in construction who had a job for me—our running joke.

Instead Zim said, "That friend of mine isn't in business anymore, so you're on your own!"

I just laughed, with a heavy sigh as punctuation. Zim knew how to acknowledge the sad part that Dad was no longer around by reminding me to laugh at myself. In the grand scheme of things—a career in which I'd come this far—sweating the small stuff was pretty silly. And yet, striking out with a runner on second may be small stuff to some, but, as Dad had taught me, the little things win and lose games. To me, giving away an at-bat was a slap in my team's face. They deserved better from me. Then again, that was my crazy logic, and Zim knew it. He'd been at this game for years, and he could size anybody up in a New York minute.

Don Zimmer was that way with me and with everyone, a force of stability in the clubhouse that commanded team respect and respect for the club's long history and tradition. This would be apparent throughout the year as the boroughs prepared to live out a continuation of that mighty tradition.

There was an undercurrent that season, almost like a subliminal drum rhythm that I could feel riding the buses and the trains. I had ridden the trains as a Reds' player, but this was different. The Number 7 train felt different all year long. The Number 4 train felt different. It was an all–New York World Series fever that had people murmuring, "This could be *the* year, the Subway Series year!"

On July 8, 2000, we had a chance to test the water with a historic split Yankees-Mets doubleheader. It was the first time since 1903 that two teams had two different games at two different sites in the same city. We played the New York Mets at Shea in the afternoon and then headed back to Yankee Stadium to play them at night. We tried to tell ourselves and the public that these were just normal games, but our own tension and the crowd fervor were at World Series levels.

We played the first game of the double-dip at Shea Stadium. Shea was rocking on its foundation, the warring camps of Met fans and Yankee fans trying to outdo, outyell, and outcheer each other.

When I walked from the bus to the visiting locker room dressed in my uniform, the atmosphere reminded me of rivalries back in high school. On the field it was much the same, the animosity heating up after we won 4–2, and we had to get out of there fast. When we walked back out together as a team, all of us en masse, the clicking of our spikes on the ground echoed in unison, as we made it from the press gate to the buses while thousands of fans stayed around to cheer us on—and to boo us.

How similar was this scene, I wondered, to scenes surrounding the Subway Series back in the 1950s when the Brooklyn Dodgers were fighting it out with the Yankees? I could almost see Jackie Robinson, Pee Wee Reese, and Duke Snider facing off against Mickey Mantle and Yogi Berra.

Looking at Zim, I was even more in awe to think he'd experienced all that. Don Zimmer had been a part of the Dodgers franchise and had witnessed the original Subway Series battles, and he loved talking about those days. He also loved looking forward in time. Zim knew we could win both games of this doubleheader (which we did) and the World Series. He had the vision.

Among the few things that could stop us would be some unforeseen injury to a key player. Another real problem that could arise would be the midseason fatigue factor—which, as only players can truly understand, can be formidable. At least that was how I saw it. My feeling is that everything about a given season evolves from spring training onward—not as just one race to the top or through games that play themselves out, but as a growth process, or a race over hills and valleys. For us to be able to win three World Series in a row, we had to travel over hills that could become mountainous and valleys that might turn cavernous. That meant playing as a team all season long, not just in the exciting launch period of a season or in playoffs at the end, but during that middle trek when the fatigue factor can be brutal on the heartiest of teams.

For the Yankees' 2000-season spring training, everyone had begun in top shape, adrenaline pushing us strongly out of the gate, continuing through May and June. The test came in July and August, because by now most players' stats for the year were established. Typically a player's stats won't change after the beginning of August—unless something drastic happens; too many at-bats have been recorded by this point for any monumental change to happen to the numbers. So now it's the everyday mode, the dangerous time of the year when pennant races are won or lost, when the psychology of looking either overly confident or lackadaisical can be a weakness. The pitfall arises when teams decide to coast and run the risk of allowing other teams to think that they are mentally and physically beatable. We didn't succumb to that trap, fortunately. Until this point we'd all been putting up the good numbers and, refusing just to coast, continued to play solid, fundamentally sound baseball. We were still Joe Torre's New York Yankees, after all.

A second wave of high-powered adrenaline came over us once again in August, as we knew we were playoff bound. That undercurrent of excitement we'd been feeling in the streets all year had become a louder buzz, with fans and the sports media starting to wonder aloud if "it" was going to finally happen this year. Just having both the Mets and the Yankees in the playoffs would give the entire city of fans their dream season—five boroughs' worth of bragging rights.

The Mets had certainly done their part. They'd played their game— also playing fundamentally solid baseball—and had made it to the postseason in dramatic fashion, clinching their league first. The Mets had won the NLDS against the Giants and then taken on the Cardinals to win the NLCS. They were in. Now we had to do *our* part. *We* had to get in.

We played Oakland in the ALDS, and it took every second of all five games to know which team would emerge victorious. The cliffhanger of Game Five was do-or-die. Scary. Not only was it played in Oakland, giving the A's a certain advantage, but we had just flown back there, playing without rest. Plus, it was a late-afternoon game with a plunging sun casting shadows that can make every outfielder go nuts. In right field the sun is just terrible until the third inning, when night has usually fallen. It can be as tough for batters who hit there regularly. If you can't pick up the ball in the glare, it's hard enough to hit it, let alone get it past the infield.

In the midst of the tension of Game Five in Oakland, Tino Martinez rose to the challenge and hit a gargantuan three-run double, giving us the lead. It was Mo time again—that exhilarating pinnacle when Mr. Lights Out sprints in from the bullpen and as an outfielder you just know the glove won't be needed because the ball's not leaving the infield. Mo, true to billing, saved the game, keeping hope alive for the next major obstacle—the ALCS against the tough Mariners.

Seattle came out in Game One and won decisively. We replied in kind for Game Two, with Bernie Williams getting a huge hit, as did Derek Jeter. We won Game Three, and then the Rocket really pitched his heart out in Game Four, striking out fifteen that day and allowing only one hit. The Mariners battled to stay alive, winning Game Five. Leading the series with our three games, Game Six was our chance to nail down the ALCS or allow Seattle to tie it up. With El Duque's magic on the mound and with David Justice knocking a three-run home run out of the park, we grabbed a 6–4 lead in the seventh inning and held on to it to win the game. When all was said and done, the night was over and we'd done our part to join our crosstown rivals in a Subway Series!

It only added to the now pounding drumroll to know that we were carrying on a tradition that had begun all the way back in 1921, when the first Subway Series had pitted the Yankees and Babe Ruth against the New York Giants.

Without a question the World Series this year was the most dramatic one of my career and by far my favorite. I felt that up there somewhere, as a spirit in the sky, Dad was looking down, watching, and loving every minute.

Yogi Berra could not have been more psyched for this championship, exulting in every aspect of it—the intensity, the fanfare, the pre-Series buildup. Many people forget that Yogi was originally an outfielder who was converted into a catcher and then finished as an outfielder. He made catching a science and was the best-hitting catcher, winning three MVP awards. Just being around him was enriching for starters, and whenever possible I also tried to get specific tips on everything I could—whether it was how to hit the outside pitch or his fielding secrets. For the World Series we were all elated to have him come into our locker room before every game, bringing with him the power of his presence and his touch of good luck.

Yankee Stadium was host to Game One—with both Yogi and Phil Rizzuto on hand. Andy pitched the opener, taking his 53–21 lifetime record at Yankee Stadium with him to the hill. Al Leiter had also been stellar for the Mets that year, and so the stage was set for a pitchers' duel.

Al allowed only two hits in the first five innings. We caught a big break when the Mets' Todd Zeile hit a dribbler that just happened to roll back into fair territory by the time Brosius came over to field it at third. He snapped it up, throwing the ball to first, and—because Zeile wasn't running at first—the throw beat him. We caught another big break later on in the game when Zeile hit a towering drive to left field, and the ball hit the top of the wall and bounced back into fair play. The Mets thought it was a home run, so they were caught in between, as the ball was thrown back in to Jeter, who made a dazzling throw to Posada to tag Timo Perez out at the plate.

A fan in the left-field stands by the name of Jack Nelson—who refrained from touching the ball—deserved applause for restraint. But then again, it turned out he was a Yankee fan, and Yankee fans know how to help their team win ball games.

Going into the ninth inning, however, the Mets were leading 3–2—just the cue for Mo to come in and hold them at bay.

It was my turn in the bottom of the ninth against Armando Benitez. Hanging in through a ten-pitch at-bat, fouling them off left and right, I wanted only to keep the at-bat alive. *Give me one good pitch to hit,* I kept thinking, *just one good pitch.* Stepping out of the batter's box after the count ran full, I wanted him to throw me a strike. Instead it was a ball. I saw it, didn't swing, and drew the walk.

Now we had one on and one out. Luis Polonia came up (playing this season for the Yankees) to bat for Brosius, and he singled, allowing me to go to second. Next up was Jose Vizcaino, who got a hit to load the bases. Knoblauch then hit a fly ball to left field, and I raced home to score the tying run.

I came up again in the bottom of the tenth, with the bases loaded, a hitter's dream. But, to my agony, I ended up grounding into a double play. After the inning was over, I was so furious with myself that I threw my helmet down on the ground. Despite my slightly reformed ways, this was the World Series—and everything mattered.

The game went on and on, and finally, in the twelfth inning, we broke through. Stanton pitched some great innings and prevented the Mets from scoring. Tino Martinez singled. Posada doubled. Jose Vizcaino came up to the plate once again, and once again he delivered big time with a single to left to score Tino and to give us a Game One victory with a score of 4–3. Even this first game of the Subway Series had made history as the longest game ever played in a World Series—four hours and fifty-one minutes.

Though I was relieved we won the game, it was no thanks to my performance. Other than the walk, I really was disappointed in my batting. For the next game, I had to have something to get me going.

As though by divine intervention, right before the start of Game Two, Yogi Berra approached me in the dugout and nodded toward my bats, saying, "Let me rub those bats for you."

This was a magical moment, unbelievable for two reasons. First, this was Yogi Berra, a baseball icon, who cared enough about me to take the effort to help. Second, I *needed* the luck—badly!

Words couldn't describe how touched I was. Not only that, but he must have charged up at least one of those bats, because I did get a hit in the game. Now I could really celebrate the Yankees' win of Game Two.

Like most superstitions, Yogi's rubbing my bats for me took on a life of its own and became our pregame World Series ritual. Before Game Three at Shea Stadium, he came over and offered, "I'll rub those bats for you." I just smiled.

Another hit. This one ripped down the left-field line—right at an important point in the game. Believe me, it was a huge relief as I flew off, hearing the voice of first-base coach Lee Mazzilli yelling like nuts as I rounded first, then second, and finally made it to third. A triple. Mazzilli had been telling me I'd have a big game.

El Duque pitched a terrific game, getting out of a bases-loaded situation. Back during one of our interleague games against the Mets, there was one unforgettable moment when he had thrown his glove—*with the ball in it!*—to Tino at first base for an out against the Mets. El Duque was that locked in at the mound and that expert at handling adversity, so he had no trouble at all striking them out when he needed to.

John Franco, however, was in his first World Series, and he was determined to shine for the Mets, which he did. Benny Agbayani got a crucial hit in the eighth to give the Mets a 3–2 lead, a lead they held.

No team in the history of major-league baseball had ever swept three straight World Series. We had swept San Diego in 1998, swept Atlanta in 1999, and we wanted the sweep in 2000. The Mets, however, stopped us, and I tip my cap to them. They got the clutch hits in the game, and Bubba Trammell gave them a 4–2 lead with a sac fly. They won the game, and our streak was stopped.

Though we were still leading the Series two games to one, there were now two more games to be played at Shea, and we were going to have our work cut out for us.

Game Four saw Denny Neagle pitching for the Yankees and Bobby Jones for the Mets. Derek Jeter started the game on a high note by hitting a home run on the first pitch, a fastball from Jones. What an amazing way to stir the Yankee fans, who were already shaking Shea on our behalf. Armed once more by bats that Yogi had rubbed, I hit a triple in the second inning, and then Brosius hit a sac fly to score me. We took a 3–0 lead in the game when Jeter tripled and Luis Sojo grounded to second base to score Jeter.

Answering in kind, Mike Piazza came up to the plate with a runner on base and gave the Met fans what they paid to see—a home run to left field. It was suddenly 3–2, and Cone came on to relieve Neagle later on in the game when Piazza was once again up at the plate.

This was also the match-up everyone wanted to see, as Cone had been a Met early in his career. Piazza flew out, and Nelson came on in relief to get a 1–3 double play that we really needed. Stanton was terrific, and then Mo entered the game.

Standing in right field, I relaxed when I saw Mo run in from the bullpen, thinking I didn't even need my glove because there was no chance of a ball's even being hit to me.

Well, apparently Edgardo Alfonso must have been some sort of mind reader, because no sooner had I thought it, he hit a sinking liner toward me. No longer relaxed, I made a diving catch to take away the hit, contributing a little breathing room to get us out of the eighth. Finally Mo came back for the ninth and closed things out.

We were up 3–1 in games, and our toughest task was ahead of us. The pressure that had been mounting throughout the Series was enormous. Even with the confidence that comes from having won two years in a row leading up to this year, and even though we were now ahead by two games, defending a title can be every bit as nerve-racking as being behind or having no recent championships. And again, this being a Subway Series, it was a championship that everyone would remember, that fans would forever tell their kids and grandkids about.

Game Five at Shea was the showstopper. Andy Pettitte was on the hill for us, and we couldn't have had a better big-game pitcher out there. Andy had been coming up strong in the postseason dating back to his earliest days, in 1996. In fact, until this point he had never given up a run on the road in all of our World Series games over the years.

Al Leiter was unbelievable for the Mets. At the plate he even dragged a perfect bunt, scoring a run himself to tie the game.

Sometimes games can be overly hyped and not live up to their billing, ultimately disappointing the fans. This game surpassed all expectations, pumping the suspense as a true pitchers' duel. Andy even picked somebody off at first. This game had it all—the drama, the spectacular plays, the New York–New York Passion squared—all the ingredients of a historic World Series game. The only thing left to be determined was the final score. Would the Mets hold on, come back, and change the momentum, or would we take it in five?

My nerves were rattled when I hit a sharp grounder to second and was thrown out at first, a really close play. A throw of the helmet was appropriate afterward, under the circumstances.

The Mets were leading 2–1 when Jeter hit a home run in the top of the sixth to tie the game. Stanton came on later in the game and gave us some much-needed innings. On the other side, Leiter was virtually unhittable. But in the top of the ninth a different energy took hold. Posada came up and really had a clutch at-bat, drawing a walk after running the count full. Brosius then got a base hit, so there were two on and two out. Luis Sojo came up and prepared to give us just what we needed at that moment.

Watching intently, Joe Torre knew it. A contact hitter, Sojo was in his element. We didn't need the long ball. We needed someone to get up there and meet the ball, make contact. Sojo did it. He hit a single right up the middle, scoring Posada and Brosius and giving us the 4–2 lead.

It was Mo time now.

Rivera came on in the bottom of the ninth and gave *everyone* the showdown they'd wanted to see all year. Game Five, World Series, Yankees ready to clinch, just one out away, and he faced Mike Piazza. Every pitch seemed like an eternity for the outfielders. We were ready for it to all be over.

And then Mike hit a deep fly to Bernie Williams, who made a graceful reach for the ball, and it was "Yankees Win!!! *Thhheeeee* Yankees win!!!!" as John Sterling called it.

There are rare moments in life and in baseball that can be described only as states of grace. This was one of those moments. For us it felt that the heavens were smiling. We had our dreams come true. The

Yankee dynasty had won the Subway Series, our third World Series in a row, and our fourth championship in five years.

It was about three or four in the morning when I made it home after the game, my heart full of gratitude, still too pumped to go right to sleep, and I was surprised when my kids came running in to see me, finding me alone having some private thoughts.

They wanted to know if I had been talking to Papa Chuck just then.

"Guys," I said, smiling and hugging them, "I *was* talking to Papa Chuck."

Nothing would ever replace Dad's being here to celebrate with me in person, but a year after his death, his wedding ring now on my left ring finger with my own wedding band, I felt his presence constantly and had conversations with him whenever I felt the need.

During the victory parade—with more millions than could be counted lining the Canyon of Heroes down Broadway—I glanced at the sky a couple of times, just to make sure he was still paying attention. And he was.

Ranking high in my top ten favorite baseball moments of my lifetime, this year had given me more than many players could want in several careers. What more could I ask for? Five World Series rings!

Another World Series wouldn't be bad, I thought. Or two.

That's when I probably made the decision, perhaps on a subconscious level. One more year of baseball, and then it would be time for a change.

TWELVE

New York State of Mind

As I look back now, from my current role as a sports analyst and broadcaster, at the decision that I faced in the off-season between 2000 and 2001, I see that part of my decision to retire came from having attained many of the dreams that had propelled my career. I'd been fulfilled beyond my wildest hopes, and there was also the fact that things were changing in baseball. Perhaps, in my baseball soul, I belonged more to an old-school era.

Of course, broadcasters have a great perspective on the ever-changing game of baseball because they sit atop the playing field and have an overall view of the game. At the same time, I have to remind myself and my media peers that the game that can look so easy on TV is not at all easy. When analysts start commenting about how they could have "made that play" in the outfield or "hit that pitch" at the plate, it becomes unfair to the players on the field. The game may appear to be unfolding slowly and gracefully from the outside view, but if a person thinks it's easy, he should try taking over right field for a day and experience how bang-bang quickly the plays are happening. The flight of the ball is not actually straight to a fielder's glove, as it may seem. Balls are hit so hard that a soft, sinking single is not so soft in reality. That single has rocketed off the bat with such force that a nonprofessional athlete would be decimated out there.

Having played the game, I continue to be amazed by plays that took place in front of my eyes—such as the bare-handed plays that Derek Jeter and Scott Brosius mastered so astonishingly. Here again, the ball is not coming at you as a soft roller; rather, the shots are all vicious and can leave a lasting sting in your hand that you still feel when the game is over. The players don't show the pain—they play through it—and the mark of their greatness is they do make it look almost effortless.

Being Chick O'Neill's son, I still believe that for fans baseball is a game that should be experienced live and in person, whenever possible. TV doesn't provide the proper perspective of the field, and it allows a view of only some of the team movement that takes place on what seems to be a simple play.

The outfield, for example, is much more vast and open than it looks when a camera angle follows the ball directly toward where an outfielder is stationed. Whenever a great hitter was at the plate, stopping the ball often reminded me of trying to cover a football field. From that angle the batter's job of trying to hit a little white ball into a sea of green seemed nothing compared to the outfielder's task of making the catch to rob him of his hit.

By the same token, the two-dimensional view on the television doesn't do justice to the challenges of hitting. Even my family members used to watch on TV and say, "This guy swings so easy."

As far as I know, there is no player who swings the bat "so easy." Every swing is the product of good mechanics and a tremendous amount of arm strength, plus the torque provided by the lower body's power. Swings may be beautiful and smooth, but they aren't ever easy.

Nor is there anything easy about throws from the mound that may look like they're secondhand to the pitcher. Never will I forget some of the formidable pitchers I faced who wore me out with their ferocity: Jesse Orosco, who was one of the toughest; Randy Johnson, who had my number; and Sid Fernandez. As a Yankee, whenever I faced Seattle, I was forced to remember that Norm Charlton knew me too well—as we had played together in Cincinnati—and it was lights out for me most of the time. The one home run I hit off him during the 1995 playoffs was a prize.

The *sound* of a game is truly what conveys baseball's level of difficulty. Dad had helped me train my ear, which as a fan is exciting and as a player is necessary. Reading the *sound* is as important as keeping your eye on the ball. I could hear the sound of the ball off the end of the bat. I heard the ball jam on a jam shot and the sound of the ball off the barrel of the bat. This was how I learned to break on a ball.

None of this is to say that TV and radio haven't improved in their coverage of the game. When it comes to the big games, the media are vital for connecting millions of fans to the game and to one another. For players, however, the glare of the spotlight adds to the demands.

Being fleet-footed was the demand that arose when Astroturf was first introduced and every team wanted fast players in the outfield. Then the long ball came back, and recently the game underwent another fundamental change in the power-hitting numbers—with many players now hitting 30 home runs per season. Game strategy drastically changed. A new era had commenced.

Part of what is required to compete in *any* era is God-given talent, and in our current baseball era especially, Barry Bonds leads the world in that category—with his recent home run record at 73! Phenomenal. He has amazed the public, fellow players, and retired legends alike.

Despite media scrutiny and unfair criticism, despite his World Series disappointments, he is devoted to his Giants, and at the plate he continues to do it all at a record pace—hits for average and for power, steals bases, and leads in walks, slugging, and on-base percentages. Barry is one of the greatest players ever to play the game, validated by his numerous MVP awards, his hitting over .300 year after year, and his status as the slugger of the modern era. From the left side of the plate, Barry Bonds gets my vote for the sweetest swing of any player I've ever seen.

Barry Bonds is the player of our era, and his mark will really be understood when the children of this generation start reminiscing about him the way old-time Yankee fans do about Mickey Mantle and Joe DiMaggio.

My sons, Andy and Aaron, will be able to tell their kids that they had the opportunity to see the likes of Barry Bonds and Sammy Sosa play.

As for the future of the game itself, from a strategy standpoint, I wouldn't be surprised if things turned around and the pitchers came back to equalize the game and reclaim the advantage. Whether this will entail coming up with a new pitch or devising new rules, I don't know, but I do think that the era of the pitcher will return, from both a marketing standpoint and a skill standpoint.

Physical demands on baseball players in all positions, for better and for worse, continue to intensify. This began with the trend in the 1990s that included both weight-lifting programs and the use of various protein supplements to give players the edge.

When I upped my workouts in the early nineties, it was important in order to keep up with the changing game of baseball, and ultimately prolonged my career and helped me through long seasons. The need for weight training and conditioning has since become an even bigger part of the game. The days of going to spring training out of shape—or just doing nothing for five months—are over. Most athletes today train year-round. They have their own gyms in their houses, and they work out every single day for hours.

Ironically, despite the improved power and stamina of the players, the new baseball era often ignores baseball fundamentals—the very same basics Dad stressed in Little League. Part of the problem is that games in the minor leagues have become something like home-run-hitting contests, and players are rushed to the big leagues.

Another problem is the way baseball is marketed, glamorizing certain star players individually rather than teams as a whole. I'm blessed to have played in an era when ballplayers were treated like kings, and so I'm appreciative, but I don't want to see the game change, from "Who won?" to "Who had on the coolest spikes?"

Generally, in all sports these days, the showboating, trash talking, and taunting have sunk to a new low. If a child watches football on television, it may seem to him or her to be about who can do the best dance in the end zone. If it's basketball, the kids see who can have the coolest slam dunk. In baseball, it's who has the best home-run trot.

Besides the pressure the media puts on this young audience to get attention in sports, I've noticed that parents are putting way too much pressure on their own children to do well. When I sit in the stands to watch my boys play Little League, I see grown-ups so obsessed with having their children outperform the others that it totally takes the fun out of the game. My jaw has dropped in amazement to hear some of the language adults will use at other kids and at their own kids.

The way parents then become competitive with one another has at times made me turn to Nevalee and ask, "Is the point here for the kids to have fun or for the parents to brag to each other?"

As competitive as I was in Little League, it was still fun, and Dad made it so. My summer baseball routine was to get up, make my bed, play in the pool all day, take a nap before the game, play it with enthusiasm, and then off to Dairy Queen for a postgame celebration dessert. In contrast, the seriousness with which Little Leaguers must train these days involves going straight from hitting school to the ball game—with separate coaches for their batting and pitching. There's nothing wrong with developing skills as an individual, but what baseball can teach, like no other sport, is a sense of teamwork and mutual respect.

My dad could not have better prepared me to become a Yankee. We won ball games as a team, which is why we had a dynasty.

And this was the team that—once I'd decided that I was playing my last year—I would be leaving. It was as scary as leaving home the first time to go off to the minor leagues. Yet I had promised myself and my family not to stay too long at the fair, to leave at the top of my game, with lots of resources of energy left to have the time to spend with my family, time that the rigors of baseball never allowed me.

Though I knew in my heart going into spring training that it would be my last, and others knew it also, I decided not to make an official announcement—knowing that the media circus would be a distraction to me and to the team.

Despite my attempt to use spring training as an opportunity to get myself into baseball shape for the upcoming show, I couldn't help feeling nostalgic about everything I was going to miss when I was gone.

For starters, there was a new kid on the block named Alfonso Soriano, who I knew was going to be a major Yankee weapon. At his first batting practice in spring training, I marveled at how quick his bat speed was and how different it was from most minor leaguers'. Many guys had come to spring training and hit home runs, but Alfonso was already on an elite level. I could tell from his wrists and hands that he was going to be a great player. He had a natural ability that was God-given, and he had speed to top it all off.

Getting to play on his team and watch him hit his stride in the next several seasons was something I was going to miss.

Nothing made me more nostalgic during the season than the realization of how connected I had become to New York City itself and how it had become such a part of me on a personal level. I was going to miss the pulse and vibe of the great metropolis, the culture, and, of course, the food. My wife and I were crazy for the New York restaurants, nine out of ten of our favorites being Italian. Besides Mulino's up in Westchester, we regularly went to Manhattan's Le Cirque 2000—where I would put on a suit to fit in with the elegant ambience and where we knew the chef, whose presentations of his fabulous dishes were as dazzling to the eye as they were to the palate. We also ate at Nino's and Il Mulino in the city. Everything about New York was the best—the shopping, the sights, the museums, the train rides. Everything we'd come to enjoy on a regular basis I would now be leaving behind. I tried not to think too much about it, because it made the move harder on me. Easier said than done.

Baseball-wise, the season had brought me some exciting milestones— including my 2,000th hit, which came during a totally lopsided game against the Minnesota Twins, one we were losing horribly. But when the Diamond Vision screen flashed that it was my 2,000th hit, the gracious Minnesota fans gave me a standing ovation. I couldn't believe that I would ever get a standing ovation for this accomplishment, much less on the road! The moment took me back to Dad's predictions after I had my first major-league hit with the Reds almost sixteen years before!

For the Yankees this season promised to be another dramatic ride, as we looked once again to go all the way—going for our fourth in a row. Mike Mussina was pitching really well this year, as he had throughout his career, and we had Soriano to add to the mix.

With the knowledge in the back of my mind that this was my last year, I could feel myself pressing at the plate. I couldn't fool myself. Sure, I wanted to go out blazing, but I should have just concentrated on hitting. I was thinking way too much at the plate.

Not that I wanted to know what was coming. That wasn't me. I didn't want to know when I was a rookie, and I didn't want to know in my final season. If I knew what was being thrown, I felt it would only mess with my mind.

Even after these many years, whenever I stepped inside that batter's box—the small, hallowed patch of real estate that has challenged many a player in front of millions of fans—there was one thought that worked for me. It was simply this: Hit the dead fastball down the middle and then adjust for anything else. If I was looking away and the ball was inside, then I'd be fooled. If I looked away and the ball was away, I still might not connect for a big shot. It didn't pay for me to try to peek at the catcher's signs, because I always thought it would work to my disadvantage.

Thinking of what Dad might have said to me under the circumstances—in the way that I often tried to imagine his positive input—I did my best just to relax, not to do too much, but to simply enjoy myself. On many occasions this season I also thought of Don Mattingly, who had so much to do with the dynasty that the team had become and whose example I followed every day. I was hoping to follow his example also in the graceful way he'd said good-bye in 1995.

By the end of August 2001, as the Yankees came into the last stretch, all of us preparing to rev up for the playoffs, I had come to terms with most of my fears and regrets about leaving. I was ready. For this last season, I was on my way to becoming the oldest player—at age thirty-eight—to steal 20 bases and to hit 20 home runs. My only concern was a stress fracture that put me in a walking foot cast and on the DL. Other than that, for all I knew, the future looked bright.

For anyone in this country and for millions across the globe, it will be impossible to forget where you were on the morning of September 11, 2001, when and how you learned of the horrific events that changed our lives and our world forever.

At our home in Westchester, it had been an everyday morning for me and Nevalee as we spent the early hours getting the kids off to school and then left at eight for the gym. Since I was on the DL and out of the series the Yankees were in at the time against the Chicago White Sox, I was putting in extra hours to stay in shape.

At the Doral Resort in Rye Brook, we had just started working out in the downstairs weight room when I glanced up at the television and saw the footage of the first plane hitting one of the World Trade Center towers. In shock and horror, we watched as the live coverage showed the second plane hitting the other tower. Nevalee and I rushed out immediately, aware that it was a terrorist attack, and hurried to get our kids out of school.

Other parents felt it was better for their children to remain in school, but we, as well as other families, thought that it was best to get our kids so that we could be together in this terrible time. We stayed glued to the television for the next twenty-four hours.

We wept to see the heroism and sacrifice amid the devastation, on the part of everyone involved in the rescue efforts—from the New York fire and police departments to those trapped in the towers who stayed behind to save the lives of other human beings to the average citizens doing everything and anything to help. We gained courage in the stories of those who arrived immediately at the World Trade Center, at the Pentagon, and at the site of the downed Flight 93 in Pennsylvania.

Mayor Giuliani, who had always been a friend to the Yankees, now became a father figure to the whole city. In a time of extraordinary crisis and fear, he took charge in an almost superhuman manner, letting New Yorkers and all Americans feel that he was speaking to each of us individually.

The team decided that we had to go down to Ground Zero to help out in any way we could. While we wore hard hats and oxygen masks, many thousands in the area when the tragedy occurred were not protected and were exposed to the poisonous air, along with the falling ash and soot. None of the team would ever forget the vision of despair we witnessed down in that area. When I visited the hospitals, there was hope in the air as families prayed that their loved ones would make it through surgery and live to talk to them again.

But at the Armory, which I visited next, it was clear that the people who were looking for lost loved ones understood that they would probably never see them again. Something happened to me at the Armory soon after I arrived that I'll carry with me to the grave.

An area had been set up with toys for children, and this one little kid was standing there. The boy ran over to me and told me how much he loved baseball, that his family was Latin American, and that he was a die-hard Yankee fan. Nodding at my cast, he said, "I hope you get back soon. I hope you feel better soon."

He then told me that he and his family were there looking for his dad. I lost it. I had to cover my face with my hands, I was so overcome. Maybe baseball gave him something happy to think about, to take his mind off the fact that there was little hope of seeing his father again. I don't know. I know that I'll never forget his face.

Curt Schilling, then of the Arizona Diamondbacks, went down to Ground Zero to do whatever he could to help. Though he wasn't a New York player and he wasn't a New Yorker, he became one during this time—connecting in his heart and in his being, just as Americans were all over the country who were grieving with New York and for those who'd perished.

The citizens of New York came together in such an outpouring of help, caring, courage, hope, resilience, and toughness that when it was decided a week later that major-league baseball play would resume—that it was our job to carry on—we as players and the rest of the country were inspired and united by that New York state of mind.

My hope is that we can remember that feeling of being united, that we will never forget the acts of heroism that came out of the ashes of the World Trade Center, the Pentagon, and the field where Flight 93 went down in Pennsylvania. My hope, too, is that we honor all those who have fought in the past and present so that America can live on, that we cherish our freedoms, and that we keep forever in our prayers the memory of those whose lives were lost.

As I think back, my memories of bidding farewell to the team and the town that embraced me are shaded by the emotions that ravaged the nation. Getting back to baseball, the fans were as amazing as ever, even more so. Despite the drastic security measures, they packed the stands—putting up with metal detectors, long waits in line for bags to be checked, even with being turned away for having bags, not to mention the fear that an attack could happen again anytime. The restrictions on player-fan interaction saddened me because—except for the time a fan had asked me to sign three watercoolers—I lived for signing autographs.

The scariest night was when President Bush threw out the first pitch at Yankee Stadium. There were FBI and Secret Service agents all over the place, sharpshooters, special government task-force personnel, and bomb-sniffing dogs. But seeing the president of the United States go to the mound alone, throw a strike to the catcher, and walk off the field sent a powerful message that the games were important for the morale of the nation.

It was hard, given all the circumstances, for the Yankees not to become the national sentimental favorites as we entered the playoffs. But the Oakland A's, winning Games One and Two of the divisional series, were playing to win. Historically, we were now in trouble. Never before had a team come back in a five-game series after losing the first two games at home. Miraculously for us, we battled back to win the divisional series, taking Games Three, Four, and Five.

In going on to win the ALCS in a hard-fought battle against the Mariners, I had the pleasure of helping in Game One with a two-run home run—a great rush for me.

My memories of the 2001 World Series are, of course, colored by the knowledge that when we began Game One against the Arizona Diamondbacks on Saturday, October 27, 2001, I had anywhere between four and seven major-league baseball games left in my life. Providing we would make it to Game Five, that meant I had only three more games to play in Yankee Stadium. Suddenly the reality of my leaving made everything that much more emotional.

Word had definitely filtered to the media, and many announcers had been making unofficial references to my anticipated retirement.

Fittingly, this series was a cliffhanger until the end—from our losing the first two games in Arizona to winning the next three at home in New York to returning to Arizona for the cataclysmic Game Six, which we lost. With the Series tied up at three games apiece, the Yankees led Game Seven—my last appearance in major-league baseball—until the bottom of the ninth inning, when the Diamondbacks pulled a rabbit from their hat and won.

Losing was secondary to the privilege and honor of playing in such a contest of great baseball and playing at such a time in the world.

These memories and many more will stay with me always. But what stands out above all the rest is what happened toward the end of Game Five of this series in Yankee Stadium—my last game played in the House That Ruth Built. We were down 2–0 in the ninth inning, our hopes were fading as I went out to right field for what I believed would be my last ever patrol of the green grass of home. Standing there, even as I paid attention to the play at the plate, I became aware the crowd was chanting something in unison—a cheer of some sort that seemed to have begun in the area of the Right-Field Faithful but was spreading throughout the stadium. I couldn't quite make out what they were saying, but the rhythm was familiar. It sounded like . . . no, it couldn't be. Was it my name?

It *was* my name. The crowd, chanting in unison, was roaring, "PAUL O'NEILL! PAUL O'NEILL! PAUL O'NEILL!"

Holy smokes, I couldn't believe it. We were in the crucial Game Five of the 2001 World Series, we were losing, and the fans were singling me out to cheer for me. Why? I wondered. Suddenly, amid the chanting of my name and the holding up of the bull's-eye signs, other signs were being lifted up that read WE'LL MISS YOU, PAULIE! and ONE MORE YEAR! They were calling out my name as a good-bye. As a thank-you.

Everything seemed to move in slow motion, suspended animation. I was in awe, a true state of grace—with goose bumps and hair standing up on the back of my neck. This was unreal, a most humbling and beautiful gesture that seemed to have happened so spontaneously. I couldn't believe that the fans of New York, after what the city had endured, would take the time or effort to make me feel so loved, to send me off in this fashion.

When at last we got out of the inning and I headed back to the dugout (for our turn at the plate that let us tie the game to come back and win miraculously in the twelfth inning), the chant was still continuing. *What do I do here?* I wondered. *How can I say thank you— without totally losing it?*

At the last moment, as I approached the far end of the dugout closest to right field, I took my cap off and tipped it in a swirl to let the fans know I was truly touched—more than that simple gesture could say, more than these words can describe.

My wife and kids were there that night, as were my brothers, as was my father's great and constant spirit.

My baseball life flashed in front of my eyes—Little League, the minors, making the majors with the Reds, getting traded to the Yankees, playing my prime years—and most of my career—for the greatest franchise in the world, the New York Yankees. Now it was over, and the future—a life outside the white lines of the baseball diamond—was unknown.

From somewhere I could hear Dad reminding me not to worry, to keep the faith, and just go out there and win tomorrow.

"Extra-Inning Stretch"

My brother Robert wrote a poem for my dad. Robert wanted to capture the feeling and emotion of a son's love for his father, and I think he did a fine job of it.

MAN ON THE MOUND
by Robert O'Neill

I

You try growing up
In Dust Bowl Nebraska
Asking your mom
When a billion locusts block the sun
"Will they eat us too?"
With a father so myopic
He beat every single thing
He couldn't understand.
How about four years of bedbugs in Panama
Guarding the Canal
From the Germans and Japanese
And machine-gunning sharks to death for dinner
Because of the rotten army chow?
He'd say, "Durn right
Harry T. dropped it on 'em,
Do the same again today."
Then he found himself pitching in Cuba in 1948
With the fans throwing bottles
Out to the mound.

Would your heart feel a little slow
When you realize in 1952
That the War took away
The best baseball you'd ever play?
No wonder he married
A tall, rich gal
In an "aw, shucks" sort of way
Who never got the dough
Though most important
She delivered all the sons
A man could want.

II

I always liked going hungry
In the morning.
But the jockey-shorted human bugle
Stood pouring Cocoa Wheats
In my breakfast bowl
Flipping flapjacks
The five hundredth Sunday in a row.
His middle finger
Pecked out all the words
"Here, Sabertooth, have another hotcake
Get tall.
It was your Great-Great-Grandpa John
Who fought the Indians
So you might live with more
But I guess a man
Lives with little
That's my phlosaphee!"

III

One baseball tournament
I tossed thirteen wild pitches in a row.
Out of the dugout he strode
Lord coach of the Little Leagues.
A funnel of dust
Led his yellow sneakers to the mound.
"You're not throwing thunder," he bellowed.
Taking the ball from me.
I went sniffling off
Kicking dust up too.
There I considered killing him
And a few hecklers in the stands
But later the Plain City Championship came
Dad sprang for hot dogs and bought the team shakes.

IV

I never saw a man
Move so much dirt
Undo a billion earthy years
Scoop by scoop
Decade by decade
With dew on the backhoe seat at dawn
Dirt puffing on him by noon
Jumping down before six
Another sun tattooed in his skin
A half day left at home to begin.
"That machine is part of my body,"
He'd wince
When Mom would demand

At the yearly fiscal crises,
"Why don't you work for someone else, Chick?"
Nothing could help him then
The small businessman
Not me at the side of the dinner table
Not even his phlosafees.

V

Tonka, our pet pony, had a toothache
So out strutted Dad
To the field in a left-handed way.
"Twenty-five bucks for a veterinarian!" he cursed.
The heat came down in heaps
And all his barefoot, sunburned sons stood back.
He propped the Shetland's mouth wide
With a roll of quarters
Out came his pliers
And a great whinny followed
His one giant yank.

VI

"What a man comes to know
Only matters for fifty years or so
But the woman knows things
That go back eons.
She lives long to advise, to advise," he said.
If you haven't figured out by now
I've got a younger brother called Ace.
Like him, I was a ten-pounder,
Born in early September.

I shifted the years in reverse again and again
Dad's middle finger taps his phlosafee
Onto the dinner table.
I'd better listen.
But the dogs are loose again
Through that fence of his
Which never got fixed.
Dad inspires me to run
And I do and I'll hunt down
Those Pyrenees polar bear muts
But never catch up
To the old left-hander.
Two thousand miles to Florida
The man drove a used van full of kids
Called it a vacation.

VII

Old Chief Bullwhip Tongue,
Thrower of the curvy words that ruled
I'll say this while you live
Because you'd certainly ask why I didn't.
You durn right this is more than thanks
Even for demanding I drive your dump truck
The morning after a Pink Floyd concert.
Real things like this
Keep disappearing from my world.

Dad's Legacy

The seasons were changing once again, in ways I'd never experienced before.

It was November when, after the last game of the World Series in Arizona, I took Andy and Aaron with me for a final trip to the locker room at Yankee Stadium to clear out my locker.

Autumn had ended much too soon; winter was on its way in. Joe Bick, probably aware that I could use some cheering up after seeing my locker emptied, phoned me. Joe had been going far beyond the call of duty as a sports agent and friend over the years, and he knew me well enough to say just the right thing to put everything into perspective.

He reminded me of an incident that had occurred in 1985, toward the end of my long stint in the minor leagues, when I was playing in Denver for the Reds' Triple-A team. Joe had come out to Denver after I'd asked him to meet a friend of mine who needed representation. While Joe was in town, he stopped by to see me at the Holiday Inn where I was staying.

How was I doing? Joe had asked.

Terrible, I said. I told Joe, in fact, that I stank, having hit only seven home runs so far in Denver.

Joe stared at me incredulously, then proceeded to inform me that I was batting .305 with 32 doubles and 74 RBIs, and that the right-field fence at Mile High Stadium—then used as a minor-league facility—was four hundred feet away. After realizing that those statistics weren't impressing me, Joe looked me straight in the eyes, warning me, "Paul, if you keep doing this to yourself, you're going to play fifteen years in the big leagues and you'll be miserable every day!"

On the phone now in November 2001, just a little more than fifteen years later, Joe Bick asked me if I remembered that day.

All too well, I said, laughing, and then I told him, "And I wasn't miserable every day!"

He was right, of course. Perfectionism comes with a price. Then again, it brings rewards: the fact that I could pack up and leave without too many regrets, hoping that what I left behind was a career that made everyone who'd ever believed in me proud.

That was again my feeling a couple of months later, in the heart of winter, when I flew in from Cincinnati to attend the Baseball Writers Association of America annual awards dinner on January 27, 2002, in New York City.

It was a little strange here in the off-season to think that the ballpark lights would be turning on once spring arrived, but that I wouldn't be here anymore. For the first time ever, I wasn't shaking hands with my friends in the media and telling them how I couldn't wait for spring training. That was bizarre. It seemed as if my first day in the Bronx nine years earlier had been yesterday. How could the time have gone by so quickly?

The night was like old home week, even though it had only been a

couple months since I'd been an active player on the team. I loved seeing everybody and wanted the night never to end, thinking they'd have
to throw me out of the hotel.

Being in the presence of Joe Torre was both the most natural thing in
the world and the most dramatic reminder of all that was changing. My
manager and father figure for the last six years, he was now my *former*
manager. Not only that, but seeing him in a tailored suit, dressed up for
the evening—out of pinstripes and ball cap—was surreal. It was much
like returning years down the road to see your high-school coach out of
uniform.

The way I would always see Joe Torre in my mind was from countless
afternoon games, the image crystal clear. There in the dugout, he
would sit watching everything on the field, his cap far down on his face
to shade his eyes from the glare of the sun—and somehow manage to
steal a moment's tranquillity while in the middle of the big fishbowl.
That's where he would be for a while to come, I figured. I couldn't
imagine him anywhere else.

That night I couldn't yet imagine that I wouldn't have a dugout to
call home. Yankee Stadium was now my former home. My locker—the
same one assigned to me on that cold day in November 1992, my
locker right up until the end—was now vacant.

Memories of my various locker-room neighbors brought other memories of great times shared. There had been Wade Boggs and Mike
Stanley, two guys who were so vital to our winning seasons. And then
there was my pal Joe Girardi—the most special of my next-door-
neighbor locker mates—who actually *lived* next door to me for a couple
of years.

When Roger Clemens arrived, he moved in to the locker on the
other side of an empty locker—which remained that way and gave the
Rocket and me a place to store excess stuff. Everything accumulated in

there—extra pairs of "lucky" cleats (just in case), memorabilia, T-shirts, protein powder, and all sorts of workout clothes.

At the awards dinner, Roger Clemens accepted his record sixth Cy Young Award, only to present it to his mom, a gesture I thought was a magnificent display of real affection. My buddy Mariano Rivera shared his Rolaids Relief Man Award with the New York City Fire Department, paying homage to their efforts on September 11 as the real heroes in America, a most emotional tribute.

Jorge Posada received the "You Gotta Have Heart" Award and spoke of his infant son's cranial operations. It had been truly heart-wrenching to see a child have to go through so much physical trauma before he can even speak. My concern remains with Jorge's son, and with all the kids out there who are suffering like him.

I thought of other teammates who had overcome many challenges. David Cone had an aneurysm that threatened his health, but he had come back strong. Mike Mussina, whose small Pennsylvania hometown had lost twenty-one Montoursville High School teens and chaperones in an airplane tragedy in 1996, had been fast to try to help. Moose knew many of the individuals who died and their families. On the field he remained tough. A go-to guy, he was somebody else I was going to miss—his teasing, his crossword puzzles, his competitive spirit.

Bernie Williams had lost his father, a loss he took very hard, but came back to rejoin the team that he knew was there for him, the team to which he gave his heart and soul.

Sitting there, I remembered what Bernie told me when he found out that the 2001 season was going to be my final one. He told me he expected me, after I retired, to come back each year for an annual jam session, with him on his guitar and me on my drums.

That was the caliber of friendship that came from the game of baseball. These were the friendships I'd be missing. I thought of El Duque,

Scott Brosius, and Luis Sojo—players who gave everything and then some, who wanted to win. This entire team, up and down the lineup, was special to me. When it came to camaraderie, our clubhouse was so tight I could see all twenty-five guys trying to ride in the same cab!

To have played in the company of such stellar baseball players and such exemplary human beings had been the greatest blessing of all.

In my fantasies I used to think about how I would've loved to have played alongside Babe Ruth, Lou Gehrig, Willie Mays, Willie McCovey, to be the right fielder while Sandy Koufax was on the pitcher's mound. Or pitchers like Bob Feller, Tom Seaver, or Cy Young. In many of my imagined plays, I dreamed of being on par with these legends, of calling these guys my teammates.

The truth is, I ending up playing on the real dream team. I know that one day names like Bernie Williams, Derek Jeter, Mariano Rivera, and Roger Clemens will be spoken in the same breath as the legends I was raised on, and I'm proud just to have been a part of it.

As the evening was winding down, Roger Clemens rose to speak. You can't help but be in awe of someone who is one of the fiercest of competitors out there on the mound. He's so set in his ways that he'll work out furiously until the day he retires. Seeing him go up to the podium, I remembered him hosting a barbecue at his home in Texas before the exhibition opener in Houston. The authentic Tex-Mex food was fantastic, and even better was the way he wanted everyone to get to know one another and feel like family.

Acting just like family this night, he looked at me with a grin. "Paul," he began, "we're going to miss you."

There was one of those quiet, touching beats right before his roast began. Roger continued, "There may not be holes in the watercooler this year, and there'll be water, but, man, we're going to miss you."

To much knowing laughter, he continued by confessing what it was like to be a next-door neighbor to me in the locker room for those years. In vivid detail he described how he learned how well I took going 0 for 5, and how I never carried that anger back to the locker room with me.

Tongue in cheek, all the way. Roger finished his soliloquy, with Yankee brotherly love, when he told everyone how my going 0 for 5 was no big deal, except that he had to take cover from the airborne objects certain to land somewhere in the vicinity of where he and twenty other teammates were standing.

Much laughter, much applause followed. Of course, hating to be the center of attention like that anyway, I was hoping a hole in the floor would swallow me up. It was all in good fun, after all. But then again, I hoped my baseball legacy—which was my family legacy—was not only about how hard I was on myself. Hadn't I already outgrown that?

For a second I thought of Robert's son, my nephew, who handles not hitting the strike zone about as well as my brother and I did when we were young.

"Stan, don't act so miserable about baseball. Dad wants you to have fun. I don't want you to be a poor sport like me," Robert once told his kid.

"I just can't help it, Dad," Stan replied. "Would you like it if your control stunk?"

The apple doesn't fall far from the O'Neill tree.

But if that was part of the family curse, no doubt intensified by the brotherly backyard competition, there was the family blessing bequeathed on us by Chick O'Neill—a true, undying love of baseball.

That was acknowledged beautifully as the awards dinner drew to a close and I was summoned to the podium to receive the Sportsman of the Year Award, as presented by *New York* magazine.

The kind words expressed about my contribution to my team and my accomplishments were as embarrassing as the roast had been. But the comments were gratifying, too, especially the recognition that, though I was a midwesterner, in my heart of hearts I would always be a Yankee—active player or not.

In fact, when not much later I was offered a job as an analyst at YES—the Yankees cable channel—it was the ideal situation, allowing me to stay on as part of the family. Because of that, when the baseball season got under way that spring, I didn't feel so left out. Not that I didn't have moments of wishing I was out on the field.

My new baseball role was fascinating, though there were times, like in August 2002 when I found myself alongside Suzyn Waldman on the field at Yankee Stadium interviewing Al Leiter, that it felt strange not to be out there taking batting practice.

But it was great getting to reminisce with Al about the Mets–Yankees rivalry that had been rekindled during my career. Al and I finally were able to laugh about those infamous Mets–Yankees games.

Al didn't let me go without reminding me of something. "What about that four-hundred-thirty-foot home run you hit off me in Toronto?" he asked.

Al is fast and crafty, and he can strike you out at any time, even in a conversation!

After the game was over that night, sports anchor Fred Hickman and my former teammate David Cone were in the studios, and Fred said, "Paul, we tried to save you some pizza." Yeah, David agreed, telling me I'd taken off too soon.

"Cone, you never saved me a slice of pizza in your life!" I said to David on the air. He just laughed.

It was fun being at the stadium as an analyst, my first location assignment. But there was still a part of me that would much rather have been out in right field watching David Cone on the mound.

Bobby Murcer, a great Yankee player and broadcaster, has often echoed that nostalgic sentiment when I've found myself with him in the press box.

Around the time that this new leg of my baseball journey began came the news that Ted Williams passed away—a blow to the fans and players who had idolized him and a loss I took very personally.

Six years earlier Don Zimmer—one of the best raconteurs in baseball—gave me the greatest compliment by telling me Ted Williams had said that he liked the way I hit. Zim swore it was the truth. It completely floored me. This wasn't an everyday high five from a peer; this was the rarest of praise from one of the greatest hitters ever to set foot on a baseball diamond. When I remembered how Dad had once compared my stance to Ted Williams's, I was even more overwhelmed. Somehow, someday, I thought it would be wonderful to meet Ted Williams and even talk baseball together. Why not dream?

Then, in the spring of 1997, as fate would have it, my sister, Molly, was working on a writing piece and interviewed Ted Williams for it. Molly talked to him about me and mentioned how much I admired him. Whatever strings she pulled, I don't know, but not long after that the telephone rang in our house in Florida, and it was him—the "Splendid Splinter" himself.

The call from Mr. Williams came at a fortuitous time. In a terrible spring-training slump, I couldn't even buy a hit and had no clue what to do about it.

"I bet you're pulling everything?" he asked in a friendly teacher tone I'll never forget.

"Yes, I am, Mr. Williams," I replied.

"You're the best when you hit the ball the other way and use the whole field," he reminded me. "So just use the whole field and hit the other way."

Incredibly, he had seen me hitting often enough to know my strengths, and he knew how to reinforce them. He couldn't have been more right. That same day, after our midmorning chat, I went out and began getting some hits, casting off the slump. This had come from a man who made hitting a science, the legend Dad had so revered.

Having had that personal contact, I was especially sad to hear that Ted Williams had died. His legacy, however, remains eternal. Few players have ever made such an impact on their peers and their fans, and he will be sorely missed by all of baseball.

It made me feel all the more fortunate to have talked to him and to have been inspired by him from the time I was very young—starting first because of my father's appreciation of him.

This summer season, full of other baseball news, was a brand-new experience for me when the 2002 All-Star break came up. When I was a player, it had long been a milestone for the season, a time when the pace of the marathon began to pick up and the leaders started to pull away from the pack. Being on the outside watching which teams were headed for the playoffs was interesting, but I can't say I didn't miss being in the thick of it.

When the first cool day came in Ohio in late August, a hint of autumn back in the air, I was pining to put on the pinstripes one more time, wishing I were there in person to see Soriano break into the 30–30 club, the only second baseman to ever accomplish that feat.

In Detroit, when the Yankees clinched a spot in the divisional series, I had serious baseball blues, missing the celebration I knew was going on in the clubhouse. It made me wonder if Scott Brosius was having similar thoughts seeing his former team clinch on television. Brosius, like me, had retired early to spend more time with his family, with his girls who were so important to him.

I saw Mo on the field and missed him. Lights Out was a major reason we'd won so many World Series championships. And then there was the Rocket, whom I missed, too.

After the game David Wells was interviewed, and hearing him, I remembered his passion for playing for the Yankees and how he loved New York City. Derek Jeter was interviewed, too, showing the same poise that he had exhibited on the field as well as in the clubhouse. Some players are defeated going 0 for 5, but Derek could go 0 for 5 and be so confident that he could get a hit in his sixth at-bat.

Under those conditions Tino and I would be sitting on the bench depressed as to when this hitless streak would end. Tino was someone else I missed.

I dearly missed the coaching personnel, whose contributions went unsung so often—guys like third-base coach Willie Randolph, who played for the Yankees and later came over to coach the Yankees and was instantly at home. A New York kid anyway, he loved being with us in the Bronx.

I saw Mel Stottlemyre on television and recalled his critical role in developing our young pitching staff, guys like Pettitte and Mendoza and Rivera. Contrary to the school of thought that says great pitchers can pitch by themselves, I believe that coaching like Mel's is essential, and I know we couldn't have won without him. Mel could read when pitchers were heading into and out of slumps, keeping the damage to a minimum. If Mel saw a pitcher having a bad start, it ended there. The respect we had for him translated into confidence and victory.

Mel Stottlemyre has yet to retire. A cancer survivor, he had shown us, as did Joe, how to be strong and overcome the odds.

There weren't even words for missing Don Zimmer and Joe Torre.

I actually missed being interviewed in a postgame show as a player. Michael Kay had been so important in helping me loosen up. Michael now had helped bridge the gap from player to analyst for me.

John Sterling, the second member of that dynamic duo, also helped welcome me to my new role. John's enthusiasm is evident—how much he cares about the game, its history, and especially the Yankees. Announcing wasn't just a job for him. His call—"Yankees win!!! *Thheeee* Yankees WIN!!"—was classic. Pure Yankees Passion. It had even evolved from an impromptu display of happiness for our club, and then the fans just wanted to hear it, so it became John's trademark.

Although I had more wistful moments, nothing could have torn me away from the new fall season I was sharing with my kids and wife. When I wasn't doing my work for YES, we were out playing together or going to ball games or watching the exciting playoffs and the World Series together on television.

That, on a most basic level, was Dad's legacy. He brought family and baseball together and used the game as the glue that bonded us and as an example of how to persevere and get the most out of a God-given talent. The journey—in the way he raised us—was supposed to be fun, inspirational, and rewarding.

To carry on Dad's legacy, I consider it as important as he did to be there for my children, to enjoy their accomplishments whenever possible—to cheer them on as students, at my son's basketball tournaments, or just as good young human beings. The older I get—and, I hope, wiser—I realize that the journey he took me on wasn't really about baseball. It had more to do with his unique way of looking at life, with a ball game or two thrown in for good measure.

Dad was a cockeyed optimist who believed that everything would work out. At the same time, he was tough, tenacious, courageous both in life and in death. Even in his last days, he never looked scared. He was taking what life was going to give him.

Chick O'Neill was no company man. He was his own man. That may have been his greatest gift, that he allowed us to be individuals. It so happened that I made it to the majors, but he never made me live up to any of his goals. The goals were mine. I never wanted to do anything else with my life other than play baseball, and I took that philosophy with me to every single at-bat in every single inning of every game in my career.

Dad's passion was me, and our special bond was baseball. The games we played, the games we saw, added up to a lifetime of learning and appreciating this great sport.

By the same token, I've tried to let my kids find their own passions and interests and have refrained from talking too much about my career with them. My philosophy is that if they feel that I'm shoving something down their throats, it will sour them on sports or make them feel they have to live up to unrealistic standards. When I'm coaching my kids, I try never to make it be about me or about reliving some glory days. Those days *were* glorious but I can enjoy them in my own memories.

This quality time shared by parents and their children—whether on a playing field or in a theater or on art projects—is a child's time to forge his or her own memories, to cultivate his or her own goals in life.

Mom and Dad, together, gave me a home and a place in which I could flourish as my own person. They sacrificed so much for all of us, for our well-being. Mom sacrificed a career in science to make sure that I had my lunches. Dad sacrificed the finer things so that I'd have a new glove.

That is both of my parents' legacy—love. There will never be enough words to thank them, though I will say it here: *I love you, Mom and Dad. Thank you for everything.*

As a moral to this baseball memoir, a story that will continue in my new adventures to come, it can be said once more that, though my father is not around anymore, I'm still his kid, and I know he's still watching over me.

I hope that you have enjoyed coming on this journey with me, and I thank you for letting me share our father-son baseball saga with you.

As a parting gift from my family to yours, I thought I'd leave you with Dad's secret pancake recipe. Perhaps you and yours might enjoy it. Remember what Dad used to say—that if we wanted to grow tall, we needed to eat lots and lots of these pancakes. It really worked in my case. Who knows, they may even have helped my batting average!

So here's the recipe for a happy Sunday pancake breakfast:

PAPA CHUCK'S PANCAKES

Hungry Jack Extra Light & Fluffy pancake mix
Egg whites mixed with corn oil or canola oil
Skim milk

Mix all the ingredients.
Add mashed-up bananas or blueberries, depending on your
    mood.
Throw in some food coloring for the kids.

It's basically the old-time, nonformulated recipe of "a little bit of this and a little bit of that"—which is why they taste so good. Feel free to adapt to your own taste and individual pancake style.

Enjoy and eat in good health!